LAST CALL

LAST CALL

The Anthology of Beer, Wine & Spirits Poetry

Edited by James Bertolino

World Enough
Writers

Poetry
ISBN 978-1-937797-06-5

Cover photo courtesy of Lorraine Healy

Editor photo courtesy of Anita K. Boyle

Book Text and Cover Design by Tonya Namura
using Gentium Basic and Gill Sans.

World Enough Writers publishes themed poetry anthologies
and special selected single- or multiple-author poetry collections.

World Enough Writers
PO Box 445
Tillamook. OR 97141

http://WorldEnoughWriters.com

WorldEnoughWriters@gmail.com

"That's the problem with drinking, I thought, as I poured myself a drink. If something bad happens you drink in an attempt to forget; if something good happens you drink in order to celebrate; and if nothing happens you drink to make something happen."

—Charles Bukowski

Table of Contents

II. Belly Up to the Bar

III. Raise A Glass

LAST CALL
The Anthology of Beer, Wine & Spirits Poetry

Introduction
By James Bertolino

This anthology has drawn poems from coast-to-coast, and while alcohol is mentioned in some way in each poem, the poems deal with a wide range of topics, issues, and experiences. It was a delight to read and select work for this spirited gathering of poems.

My memory of the first time I had drunk an entire can of beer seems like a good way to introduce this anthology:

Having Beer with Grandpa—a little personal story

When I was fourteen, and my brother twelve, our parents sent us to the village of Pence in northern Wisconsin (we lived in Stevens Point, right in the middle of the state) to spend a week or so with our paternal (Italian-born) grandfather.

We didn't know then that Grandpa had come to America when he was fourteen—to work in the iron mines. His parents were both dead, and he'd supported himself in Italy by being a young miner. At that time, American mines were hiring Europeans with experience and paying for their passage to this country.

About the second or third day of our visit, we'd run out of things to drink, and Grandpa asked us what we'd like. Before I could open my mouth with "Coke," my brother Dennis shouted "Beer!" Gramps was okay with that, and for our next meal he provided a six-pack.

As we sipped our beers from the cans, we chatted. And as my brother and I felt more and more relaxed, we began to ask him questions. We learned things about Grandpa, and he learned things about his grandkids. It was the first time I realized that a little alcohol can loosen things up. When we returned home, it was with the realization that alcohol isn't about getting drunk, it's about having an interesting, and lively time.

We told our parents about drinking beer with Grandpa, and that may have been one of the reasons Mom and Dad began to serve small glasses of wine to us, and our two older sisters, at every holiday meal. We felt so grown-up!

And now, a toast to all the writers, and readers, who will spend time with this book:

The Toast

May you always have art to charm
your days, a sensible hearth,
and friends as dependable as gravity.
May the wind and creatures be as music
to your evenings alone, and may your dreams
leave you renewed. May you have an appaloosa
to ride the outline of blue hills, and nothing
that sickens, and no black sticks.

Cheers, ¡Salud!, Prost, Cin-Cin, Santé,
James Bertolino

I. Odes & Other Poetic Libations

Patrick Dixon

Idle Dreams

Imagine all the waters of the sea
somehow transformed magically:
and instead of salt-water brine,
the waves all were made of wine!
Port or red or chardonnay
would be the best feature of cove and bay...
gulfs of burgundy and seas of zin:
it's a world I could live within.

But this fantasy's not entirely clear:
I'd really rather see water turned to beer!
Rivers of bitters run to lakes of mead?
That'd be quite a sight indeed.
Imagine the foam we'd see in the lakes
as boat props churned malt in their wakes.
Oceans of lagers, weisens or stout—
we'd get depressed as the tide went out.

There's some advantages to this plan
that could come in handy for the average man:
What do you think would unlock her heart?
Cook Inlet full of bock is a damn good start.
A creek full of amber is good for what "ales" you,
or a dip in a backyard pond of hoppy home brew.

I guess I'd be sad if this actually came true
'cause at day's end I wouldn't need a brew.
No, I'd rather share a drink, you see
with friends like you—after goin' to sea.
Tell stories and yarns deep into the night
and shake 'em and stir 'em til we get it right!

But mixed drinks are for different cheer—
right now it's high time for another beer.

Glass of Rye

The ebbing rye tide
reveals the cherry's top
like a slowly emerging shoal
as the sea seems drunk
by the moon.

Glinting liquid shot through
with burning eyes as it flows
over the fruit's curved surface
to settle into crystal vertex.
Five floors up, our bar's neon
winks above Portland's hunkered
rooftops. Waves of *hellos*
and look-at-me laughter rounds
out a room punctuated by glass
cracks and ice clinks.

Cherry emerges fully; speared
with plastic sword and eaten,
glass emptied. Whisked away,
the clear orb scoured and stored
with its necklace of mates
in the bright-lit shelf below
bottles winking Versailles
colors, promising evanescent
insight as that last fiery tear
is swallowed.

Sheila Nickerson

On the Career of Cherry Wine, a Racehorse

Cherry Wine ran second in the Preakness,
then faded to seventh in the Belmont Stakes.
It's like that with cherry wine—
so much depends on soil, weather,
and conditions of the heart
as you start to crush the cherries,
pouring in every win and loss.
To make the finish you must be strong—
bold as a stallion, but sweet as summer fruit.
Remember, you were born to run this race.

Fruits and Berries

We have gathered our fruits and berries,
Vetted and vatted them until crisp and clean.
They lie now in state hoping to replace
Hard tension of tannin with fragrance
And body of esters you respond to.

It takes time. At least a few days on their own.
Racking has been hard. Dregs always a drag
With labeling taking much saliva.

We could meet early next week if you wish.
There's no net to the internet.
Besides, I could decant or recant
At your pleasure. Yours very truly...

Aaron J. Silverberg

Exquisite

delivering food farm finder pamphlets
I visit a tasting room where she pours me
what she calls a "liquid PB&J"

I smile at the allusion, but once the combination of
hazelnut wine and cassis, dance on my palate
I'm in love

"that's ... exquisite"
and I sip once more to make sure
ah elucidation

the reduction of a field of hazelnuts and black currant
to a proof of divine existence
reminds me why I stepped away
from the trough of philosophy
to imbibe the essence of poetry

Sara Levinson

Ode to Wine

How delightful is the feeling of wine!
The first taste and then
the slow gulps,
the way it fills the cup and
delights my nose,
and slowly how it
replaces anxiety
with beauty,
and how funny all the jokes become!
How the simplest people become so damned *interesting!*
How I can't get enough of their banter!

How it warms the insides and
how beautiful the music and laughter
that linger in my ears,
how good the air feels,
how careless and irresistible each gesture!
How long and endless the night—and yet,
here ends the bottle of wine.

Luther Allen

white snow and red wine
more white snow and more red wine
less every sip

Wine Stains

A favorite book,
On every page,
A shying intensity.
Brown, not like the grape,
A raku cup.
On the lip,
A potter's trick,
A painted crack.

I flip
Through a quick cartoon,
A kiss,
A wrestler's rabbit punch,
To watch the spot reduce,
And in reverse,
A growing blot.

The stain regains
Its liquid self,
Here at the moment
Of spilling.
I can't recall
The cause or setting.

The dog of anger's kick,
An accident of overeagerness,
Alas, what might
have ensued instead?
An easeful unrest,
A grammar of hesitancy
Of word and breath.

Pinot noir, a note
Dropped on the floor,
A girl.
A fiction unfurls.
Was there wine, at all?
Or even a glass?
Did I buy this book
Already dyed and pressed?

James A. Gollata

In Vino Triage

The EMT
In urgent ease
Opens a bottle, says
Breathe, Damn You! Breathe!

Ellaraine Lockie

Dinner Date

I asked how he felt
about sharing wine
Would he put his lips
on the rimmed rust brown of mine
a few seconds between sips

He took my glass
Swirled the red Zinfandel
Sniffing it twice
And said he'd thirst in hell
before drinking Revlon's Autumn Spice

Wine Fest

This flock of apostolate souls suffers
Saint Swivens style
under July sun
and hangs grail-holding
lanyards round sweaty necks.

So begins the dusty pilgrimage
for sweet and acid sacrament—
offerings of
Sanguis Christi Cabernet,
Adoratio Bordeaux,
Liturgia Verdi Chardonnay—

From station to station,
tannins and heat elevage
into swaying visions and
temptations for the label's mark
from the Kiss of the Devil.

Funnel cake shared,
heat and sun receding,
we cloister
near Porta Potty purgatory
before heaven-sent transportation arrives.

David Radavich

Shiraz

It is a drink
the color of blood—
divine
and life-giving.

War has been
ripened and plucked,
aged and tested—

sun
and shadow

now swirling
around
nose and lips,

a seduction
of soul,

last dance
of the demons.

The Rapture

This red goes down easy, too easy.
I'm on my second glass.
My husband pours, *Say when,*
and fills my glass to the rim,
I tell him, we need bigger glasses.

This is the kind of wine you can chew:
grapes, plums, chocolate covered cherries.
So soft, so luscious, cells swagger your brain,
a distinct heat flushes your skin.

And, upon taking another sip of these miraculous
molecules—I imagine the same particles Jesus turned
water into wine. The same blood you take with the body
in communion after blessings from the Priest,
as he places one desiccated wafer of forgiveness
upon your tongue.

When you drink this wine, you believe
the Holy Spirit has visited upon your house.
And you know how climatic it must feel to be saved,
to speak in tongues and to rise up in glory
when the choir sings, *How Great Thou Art.*

Nebbiolo
Ottava rima

These purple grapes from Barolo,
harvested soon after first frost,
are kissed by the chiaroscuro
of October's creamy fog. Lost
in the vapor, a milky kimono
veils each orb. These ghost
grapes give us Nebbiolo wine.

Sip, and believe in the divine.

Wine

Pliny the Elder

… the infant who resolved
    at Saguntum to climb
    back to his mother's womb:
    that place burned that year, at the hands of Hannibal.

    Lacking this
end to endless
appetite I
    fill a glass, my tremulous
    hand unable to hold the over-
flowing vessel: a glass
        within whose swirling forms
        a formal banquet room—
I see red veins on the cheeks of Caesar:

    on that map
the weak, thin wine
of empire spreads
    as his wife takes her bath for hours
    in the milk of half a thousand asses.
Serving unspeakable thirst—
        the hand at the nipple,
        the finger on the rim
begs for an end to nothing, and nothing holds.

Cenobite

Come dawn, he lifts his tonsured pate,
dons his frock, and hauls his paunch
past chapels with carved overmantels,
down the dizzying caracole leading
underground to a hive-like vault where
malted barley and hops are alchemized into beer
and honey and water fermented into mead,
plenishing metal drums as kirsch, perry, and cider
distend oaken barrels and casks
under the scrutiny of the manciple and cellarer.

He avails himself of provisions designated
for members' immediate use, filling
flagon, decanter, and carafe to their brims
with a devotion spirituous if not spiritual,
ever grateful for a convent's conveniences.

Sated, he rouses himself at noontime
and warmly receives mendicants,
friars of every order crowding the almonry
for a taste of nectar, dispensing with askesis
for the sake of sampling the World to Come.

Cale Budweiser

5000-year-old Beer Discovered

Before Confucian *Analects* and Taoist anecdotes,
upon the Central Chinese plains, 5000 years ago,
shaped funnels, pots and jugs were found that brewed
    and filtered beers,
produced with broomcorn, millet, barley, tubers and
    Job's tears.
Some archaeologists at Stanford University
have analyzed an ancient residue discovery;
a stove for carb-to-sugar breakdown was found at the
    site,
and ion chromatography was used to test its bite.
The evidence showed grains were damaged, malted
    and/or mashed,
but quite a happy hour when the liquid-gold was cached.

Ode to a Stout
appassionato

Oh, black thou stout!
Opaque Lethe of midnight oil,
heavy syrup of ferment,
thine ABV obliterates me.

Crown of brown-cream lather
sunk in a snifter, legs
a thousand miles long—
Niger goddess, I drink thee,
lap the ebon ripples of
thine oracle pool, my
glass a bulb of torpid
frothing tar fruit.

Aflame liquid,
burn thou me
well, stout!
No errant cry
of *lager, pilsner*
or *simpering ale*
escapes me—
abliss these lips,
mudded with thine
earthen sacrament.

Maenad

She comes in every afternoon
And asks me to pour her a glass of heirloom jewels;
Rubies and garnets still warm
From lying against the hearts of the dreaming
    departed.
And I fill her polished glass with yesterdays.
Their roots twist through ancient battlefields
Nourished by the blood of visionaries with impeccable
    timing
And scarce potable water.
And she sits with me a while and perfumes my day
With the smoke of bridges burned,
With pepper spilled from her enemies' wounds,
With chatty violets that lift voice in her every gesture.
The sight of her,
Handsome and rich and supple,
Goes down smoothly,
Warming without burning,
Drying my throat,
Then revitalizing like a handful of stolen berries eaten
    in solitude.
And I would live with her in that glass,
If she would make room for me to swim with her
    secrets.
She lingers always for a single pour;
One, and one only, taken daily,
Then carries my gift home on her lips,
The taste of red diamonds,
And leaves me feeling as if we've kissed.

Daniel Weldon

We're Too Good of Lovers to Be Friends

Stuck with a memory of how you taste
How my and your mouth mix
Kissing sangria and red lipstick
It bites my tongue again
We're too good of lovers to be friends

I'm drinking whiskey like water
Feeling that familiar twist
It's the speed and crash I'm after
An explosion ending where it begins
We're too good of lovers to be friends

We'll call it passion play
We'll call it chemistry
We'll say, "I love you" sincerely
Then we'll quietly slip away
Looking back to where the pavement ends
We're too good of lovers to be friends

Into our lives miles apart
And a road well-worn traveled on
Blissed, wrecked, a bit sad at heart
Knowing both who's here ... who's gone
Smiling at how easy it is to pretend
We're too good of lovers to be friends

Victoria Doerper

Old Wine, for My Husband

A young grinning Beaujolais
Splatters insouciance.
On new lovers in new skins,
Fans up the fleet sparks of youth
For awhile. But we demur
The mad dash for that fresh girl.
We, old lovers in old skins,
Don't mind waiting for the fire.
Rough tannins tumble smooth,
Raw lust sculpted into strong
Chiseled angles of desire,
The genre poetry, not news,
Stays true beyond the first
Season. We will reach the last
Vintage one of these days,
And pour what's left of ourselves
In silky sigh of transmuted fruit
Like a spill of seasoned Cabernet,
Clear ruby sparkle, grape spent,
Bottle empty, lees left behind.

Carly Sachs

A Drinker's Love Poem

I could drink the glass of you down,
the vodka of you—
how you can lose yourself in anything,
the woo-woo of you, the kamikaze
of you, the fuzzy navel of you.
The rocks of you melt into another
round, the Maker's Mark of you,
the martini, dirty of you, the extra
olives of you, the Sapphire eyes
of you, the Effen body of you,
the make it a double of you
until we order tequila shots past
the midnight of you, no salt, no limes,
the pure scotch of you, the peaty
sex of you, the my father of you,
the Freud of you, the Oedipus of you.
Mornings of bloody mary sting of you,
afternoons of the perfect manhattan
of you, the sleepless city of you.
I want the distillation of you, the fermentation
of you, the rim of my finger
on the glass of you.

Jackie Craven

Thirst

I promise him everything—rivers, falls,
Lake Saguaro—but he sniffs and turns away.

Weeping and pleading, I follow him
across the mesa. I fling my arms
around his hollow neck and he becomes a snarl
of tumbleweed.

His teeth are salt and heat has shrunk his eyes.
All he needs I can give, and still
he hurtles into the yellow wind.

Leah O'Sullivan

April

I want to get drunk on spring,
on a sky open like a loved one's arms.
I want to bloom and buzz,
drinking dripping nectar
and tasting scattered pollen.
I want to breathe in the breeze
and breathe out something fresher than
vodka stale on my tongue.
I want my blood to flow like
a river through cracking ice,
to move my body toward the blue sky
instead of down into bed where
my dizzy head wants to rest, alone,
watching the room spin.

Paul S. Piper

Blue Curacao

It was in her eyes and
we were swimmingly in it

togetherest. Enough like
cuckoo to make us thus.

We were an island of blue
In a sea of blue, awash

with waves of blue
and sand of blue.

Bottle in the center
of the Gabbeh rug (blue

since you ask), half full
of blue, half the path

we'd taken. Scattered
clothes, scattered leaves,

it was Autumn after all
and we were hot and blind

and in the blue fury of it.

33

John Davis

Swirl the Spirit

Nose the whiskey. Note the spice
of nuts and vanilla lingering on the rim.
Taste the sweet streak of corn against your palette.
That's the leafy-grassy-haylike

scent of malt, the woodsmoke tar,
the golden-amber-copper hue
shot through with mauve and rose,
or maybe the henna hue has hooked you

or mahogany lights up your glass.
Swirl the spirit. Look at the tears
adhering to the sides.
You're creamy, fuzzy or fizzy.

You're fresh-smooth-coarse-light and heavy.
You're rich. You're mellow.
You're maturing in an oak cask
and you're getting drunk.

Susan J. Anderson

Triolet: Dutch Courage

I possessed guts and spunk,
    then got drunk off my ass.
I saw through the bunk
of a burden-filled funk;
until youth from me shrunk
    and drowned in a glass.
I possessed guts and spunk,
    then got drunk off my ass.

Sneak, Sneaked, Snuck

He's trying to say his words just right as he slips
into bed and paws her waist to wake her up,
changing his mind about quiet
after failing badly to sneak in,
clomp, clump, bang, thud, switch
the bathroom light on and a beam across the bed,
oops shit, didn't mean to do that,
brushes his teeth, swish, swish and spit.

He's trying to conceal how much he's had to drink
—drink, drank, drunk, hey, he can still conjugate
the verb right in his head—so maybe
he's not so badly wasted, just
a couple of beers, not mentioning they were pints,
and a very small glass of wine, four fingers high,
he'll show her if she asks, but don't mention
the Scotch to top it off, do not mention that.

He's trying to wrap
his mouth precisely around his intentions;
the vowels, that's where you hear the drunk,
he thinks, so enunciate like hell.
But whole syllables get left out he doesn't notice,
and here his voice rises like a girl's
and speeds way up, defying his floppy tongue
and drink-sedated lips,
and there's another sibilant gone bad; he almost
hears it blurring, and knows she's listening
—can you say like a hawk or an owl in the night
she's listening—nothing gets past her, he's doomed.

But if she says he's tanked, he'll say,
no, no, just half, but then he merrily blurts out,
I'm glad you're not a state trooper.

He thinks now probably she's got him pegged,
and maybe he's got her crying
as she's shaking a bit under his mitt,
until she bursts out with her merry laugh
and he cringes for the blow, and there, she says it, done.

But it doesn't come out as bad as he'd thought,
because what she says is, *you're squiffed, tonight,*
my love,
and it's the first time she's said those words to him,
my love, just plain like that,
and that's when he falls asleep,
snort and snore, beside her,
not to remember tonight in the morning,
asleep content that something very welcome
has snuck into his dreams.

Kyle Potvin

After Hours

Say goodnight, amygdala.
Seep well in gin, vermouth and bitters.

Shut the mind's blinds
Against the bloody and the sour.

Brush off despair
With your toothbrush

And swallow prayers
Like water.

What does it matter?

In the morning,
You'll remember nothing.

Judy Barrat

Coffee for Wine
a/k/a/ The Morning After Poem

Oh to taste that first cup of coffee
    After a night of revelry divine—
Of dining and dancing and corner romancing
    And wine, yes, the ruby red wine.

Oh the scent as it floats down the hallway
    Is the rooster announcing the sun
To a brain in decline from the ruby red wine
    But I'd drink it again for the fun.

Oh hear it drip-drip through the filter
    Filled with lovely ground french roasted beans.
If it weren't for the wine, I'd get to it just fine
    But my legs tell me: "find other means."

Oh bless the solid walls that now guide me
    As I follow the scent of dark roast.
Next time I'll decline the ruby red wine
    But right now—please—some coffee and toast.

Oh auto drip pot on the counter
    Gurgling and sputtering my name—
I'd respond gleefully if only I could see
    But the wine's left me blind and quite lame.

Oh Lord, put a mug in my hand now
    And if you help me in filling it too,
There'll be no more dining with ruby red wining
    I shall stick with my french roasted brew.

Drowning My Sorrows

I try to drown my sorrows
but my sorrows can swim.
They backstroke, splash
in a pond of tequila.
So I make a lake
of bourbon. They laugh,
play Marco Polo. Next,
an ocean of vodka.
They float on their backs.
Oh, I know my sorrows
are little sorrows
compared to the horrors on TV.
But damn, they're resourceful.
Some use ice cubes as rafts.
They even work together,
bigger ones hoisting
smaller ones on their shoulders.
I look down into the glass:
my father's last words,
my neighbor's face
after his grandson blew up
in Iraq, my widow mother
alone in her house
talking to photos;
and, of course, scars
from my divorce,
little life preservers other sorrows
cling to (What have I done?
Oh, my poor children).
I add rum, gin,
tidal waves, tsunamis.

Pour some wine,
no ice cubes this time.
They vanish and for awhile
I can breathe.
They hold their breath.
Their tiny heads bob
like buoyant corks,
mouths agape.

Pantoum

The recurrent sound
a matchbook extinguishes
too quickly life goes by
bottles pile in the recycle bin

a matchbook extinguishes
and another bottle appears
piled atop in the recycle bin
booze aficionados pontificate

and another bottle appears
luminescences of microbrew
booze aficionados pontificate
from blonde to auburn to brown

and luminescences of homebrew
to be this hopped to party
in blondes and auburns and browns
how our carnal tastes abound

to be this hopped a party
life goes by too quickly
while our carnal tastes abound
ears tuned to the recurrent sound

Sam Wagner

Death at City Tavern

He cried because he wished to be out of tears.
So he drank, though they would not run out of beers.
He didn't accomplish very much before he died.
His tears rolled back into his glass and
he drowned on the endless supply.

Sam Wagner

The Beer Not Dranken

Two beers remained whence came last call
And sorry I could not afford them both,
Being just one drinker, long I tried to stall
And discern from one label anything at all.

Then ordered the other, split the pair
And having perhaps the better name,
Implying, I thought, a less hoppy beer.
Though as for that the other one there
Had been brewed about the same.

And both that evening, I must say,
The two were hard to discern.
Oh, I kept the first for another day!
Yet knowing how heavy beers can weigh,
I doubted if I should remember to return.

I shall be slurring this with a sigh,
somewhere lagers and ales hence:
two beers remained behind the bar, and I—
I drank the one less drunken by,
But I got just as drunk.

Frank Wright

A Mountie From Brunswick

A Mountie from Brunswick named Bruce,
Encountered a crotchety moose.
He dined on its meat,
From the nose to the feet,
And made beer from the leftover juice.

Bruce Berger

Beer and Bier

The inaugural buzz
Formed adolescent bonds
With all the choice there was,
Cheap American blonds.
No wonder I was awed
When suaver friends would proffer
Lagers from abroad.
Brew had more to offer.
Then a revelation,
Artisanal, craft,
Sprang from our very nation.
In retrospect I laughed
At swill I once had swallowed.
My taste was growing darker.
Amber quickly followed,
A transitory marker
To my present grail,
This palate's chosen dodge.
In India pale ale,
Subcontinence of the Raj.
In sum, a tasteful journey,
Sampling all that brewers
Wheel out on the gurney,
This one mine, that yours
As time for cheer grows shorter,
And past the penultimate stout
Awaits a final porter
To usher the way out.

Diane Stone

Revelry

The family cat snug in her plush black fur
snoozes near the fire, gently snoring,
committing every ounce
of her corporeal self to earthly comfort.
My husband on the sofa
inhales the heady fumes of Tolstoy's words.
He lowers his book to inform me
that Napoleon has taken Moscow
and winter's hard, blunt wheel has turned.
Then he looks away, eyes skidding
back into Russia's supreme snow.

Staying home with cat, book,
glass of wine is revelry enough.
We've had our share of celebrations
and disappointments too.
Out in the dark, cold space of time
cheerful revelers drink and dance;
midnight flares from zone to zone
until the sash of earth fades
and the new year rises like a golden crown.

Our cat stops snoring when I nudge her
with my toe. My husband keeps reading,
torn between New Year's Eve with me
and the glittering fireworks of Tolstoy.
Tonight he chooses Leo Nikolayevich.
So for this reveler a second glass of wine,
rich and red, and a toast to the old year,
a great doomed hulk
that lists starboard and sinks.

Reincarnation

Who would believe in reincarnation
if she thought she would return as
an oyster? Eagles and wolves
are popular. Even domesticated cats
have their appeal. It's not terribly distressing
to imagine being Missy, nibbling
kibble and lounging on the windowsill.
But I doubt the toothsome oyster has ever
been the totem of any shaman
fanning the Motherpeace Tarot
or smudging with sage.
Yet perhaps we could do worse
than aspire to be a plump bivalve. Humbly,
the oyster persists in filtering
seawater and fashioning the daily
irritations into lustre.
Dash a dot of Tabasco, pair it
with a dry martini, not only
will this tender button inspire
an erotic fire in tuxedoed men
and women whose shoulders gleam
in candlelight, this hermit praying
in its rocky cave, this anchorite of iron,
calcium, and protein, is practically
a molluskan saint. Revered and sacrificed,
body and salty liquor of the soul,
the oyster is devoured, surrendering
all—again and again—for love.

Martini

I like to sit with E.B. White's *elixir of quietude.*
at the end of a hard day, but

I prefer mine classic—
straight up with an olive. Never dirty.

And *please* do not stuff the olive with anything
other than the pimento it was born with.

(Though sometimes I desire the kiss
of a twisted lemon.)

Depending on mood,
I'll take either vodka or gin

with a whisper of vermouth:
think vermouth over the glass, or

look at it across the room,
the way Churchill liked to do.

The vodka must be *Grey Goose* or *Absolut* or
Skyy in the electric blue bottle,

but I'm not fussy about the gin.
Bombay Sapphire or *Tanqueray.* Something smooth.

Don't let Mencken's *only American invention as perfect
as the sonnet* languish in the shaker diluting,

losing its crisp astringent essence;
and never call it a vodkatini or kangaroo.

"Martini" is not a synonym for cocktail.

It is not sweet. It is not
an apple, chocolate or pineapple-tini.

Don't add liqueur or sugar or champagne.
Don't turn it into a bubbly girly drink.

Don't ever think it deserves the name *martini*
if it's orange or pink.

Let's raise a martini toast, dear love!

Martini

Scent of juniper berry,
modulated fire,
after a day's excursion
across my Cubist
calendar, I reach
for your breast-
tapered, long-stemmed
quietude.
I want to dissolve
self into smooth sea,
efface the horizon,
greet the setting sun
exultant, sultry
& unbuoyed.
Sing to me now
of the golden
Riviera,
the abundance
of forest
& opulence
of meadow.
Persuade me
with your chilled
transparency,
instruct me
with the wisdom
of your olive-green
eye.

Martini

Look how the olive green sun
slowly slips into the cold shimmer
of a glass of gin, the evening sky
beginning to glow red as pimento
behind the blue hills. Clouds spread out,
delicate as cocktail napkins, and the birds
begin their scat of warm-up trills,
vibratos, little snips of phrases.
I can hardly wait to see
that evening sun
go down.

Patricia Wellingham-Jones

Cocktail Hour

For thirty years
they have sat together
as day fades into evening

Lifted glasses in toasts
smiled over triumphs
raged or wiped tears
over plans and people that sank

Today at his elbow
a cut-glass tumbler
filled with red wine
the color of hummingbird throats
diluted with water
and a trail of mucous down the side

In Alice's hand
a crystal tumbler
of scotch over ice
barely watered
retaining the golden hue
of dried gorse and bracken

Wine abandoned
he dozes
head falls on chest

Alice wonders where wonderland went
picks up her novel
reads a chapter or two
Refills the glass of scotch
before heating dinner

Sheila Farr

Long Night

I drink to drown my sorrows, but.
the damned things learned to swim.
—Frida Kahlo

There'll be no cocktails in the afterlife,
so let's stir one now as the season
resurrects old sorrows. While the moon turns
its blind eye and seeds knuckle-under
in December's chill, why not?

Let's have a drink, as Earth's orbit
wrings the last sip of daylight
from this fickle year. In a photograph
of old companions, I tick off
the dead. Icebergs crumple.

Sulk, sleep, weep if you must; there's
devilry atwitter. Our quavering sun slinks
below the horizon. Crows flee.
When night falls, time unravels. So dance,
whirl, as the heavens reel.
Solstice is near.

Rosalie Calabrese

Oenophilia

A fancy word for simple pleasure,
strong as beaujolais, soft as chardonnay.
I can get higher on a sunset,
yet each night I raise a glass of chablis
to celebrate day's end,
toast tomorrow's mystery.

Timons Esaias

The Alcoholic Beverages of India

The name Arrack
tells nothing
of how the stuff
tastes

Just as the word
whiskey
gives no idea—
smell of burning crofts—
of the range of it
nor really
does the formula—
centuries of pain—
for arrack

Words have only meanings
that one already knows
or thinks one knows
and mystery—
Sura, Pali, Pendhā,
Andhra Pradesh Kallu—
from what we suspect

Language needeth
one more power
needeth to summon
the thing it names
the very thing
for then it can tell
finally

what you
did to him
and how it was
all my fault

Aged Together

What began in the day of Mateus Rosé
settles into the evening of bourbon and scotch;
less now the sweetness, more the slow burn, and such
complexity that neither love can say
what flavor comes from which charred cask,
what overtones of caramel and smoke
come from which life, what ancient oak
location, heat or cold, what jeweled flask
has made us what we are: *dignified*,
they say of whisky, *subtle, rich,*
not *youthful* or too *big*, with perfect pitch,
an old torch song of booze, and on the side
a glass of ice and water waits to cleanse:
a shock of everyday as the poem ends.

Anthony Beal

Little Apples of Sanlúcar

Good evening, my longtime friend.
Come shake my hand
In that secret way nearly as old as us.
Sit with me and enjoy this salty air.
Once more let us relive past struggles and losses;
Let us catch and release brief glimpses of youth.
We'll eat them with nuts and olives.
We'll drink them with *jamón* and *fruits de mer*,
Then lift our glasses of acquired wisdom
To Pedro and surrounding shores
Where ancient horses wear their colors with pride.
We'll go down dry as uncounted years foretold.
We'll rise with mouths full of chamomile,
Feet rooted to the ground
In the boots of our grandfathers,
And dance fleeting *cante jondos*
Like the new old men we have become;
Blood brothers,
As filled with stars as the night above.

Barbara Crooker

The Wine Tasting

The connoisseurs meet to drink and compare,
roll redness on their tongues,
inhale the heady air,
rate and bicker.
Watch them make their lists:
there's a noble Lucent
and a crisp Charisma, estate-bottled.
Perhaps they'll include some old Patina
or a robust Lamborghini.
What about a Raddichio—
such a prominent nose!
Or sweet liqueurs—
a golden Mellifluous,
a delicate Gallinule.
Around the oaken library table
they sit and compare
weigh and measure
the savor and bouquet
of such a chosen few:
a Roseola '68
an Annelid '80
or a Clairvoyant from any even year.

Tina Schumann

Seven Ways of Looking at a Corkscrew

Oh, you little purveyor
of necessary violence,
always drilling towards the sweet stuff.

Domestic augur, supplier of sin
and swirl. I love you.
I love you because

you make me say the words;
Montalpulciano D'Abruzzio,
Pinot Noir, Barbaresco.

Oh, tool of ancient knowledge,
minimalist of the pull and pop.
Cool and steely under pressure.

Teach me to float above the vine.
Give me reason to be hard.
Train me to lie dormant in a glove box.

Oh, you one trick implement
so happy to oblige.
How have I discarded you?

Took you for a con?
Blamed you for my habit,
and thrown you to the drawer.

Praise be to you and the cork;
a partnership sublime and mature,
adults in an adult situation.

Let us make a bond today—
I will succumb to the juice
and you will mark the way.

Lynn Hoffman

Drinking Song for Poets

Here's the reason poets drink:
it thaws their eyes and lets them blink;
and when poets blink, they sometimes hear
the muses singing in their beer;

and blinking then, the poet knows
the smell of lyrics in his nose;
or sometimes red wine can reveal
hot visions of how poets feel;

drinking long and drinking well
matures that ripe poetic smell
if they drink with a just poetic touch,
not too little, not too much.

Highbrow poets over-drink
(it's even worse than people think).
Some lowbrow types avoid the stuff
(it interferes with writing fluff).

But the brewers' gifts are best bestowed
on stalwarts who can bear the load;
who take from Bacchus what they need
and write the songs that people read.

So let's open up a magnum now
for a poet of the middlebrow,
a liter and a half or maybe three
to water his glib facility.

Or a cork and cage-cap flask of beer
and bring it quickly over here!
It's very late, there's little time,
let's hope the rhyme is worth the wine.

Carol Gordon

What Happens at a Cocktail Party When Someone Asks Me What I Do and I Answer, "Poetry"

There's the pregnant pause.

The calibrations of adjustment
behind his eyes, the effort
to look focused.

The others in our circle
poke their olives, or swirl Merlot.

Because I feel particularly
what-the-hell, I say
nothing, and wait for,

"...What *kind* of poems
do you write?"

Devil-take-the-hindmost,
I reply, "The best I can."

He means, he counters,
    "rhymed or humorous,"
he hesitates to mention love.

Relieved, our listeners skulk off
for refills.

He's saved me from myself.
He winks a wink conspiratorial:

    "I wrote one once, myself."

Jane Blanchard

Uncorked

When buying wine,
imported or domestic,
I rarely find reviews,
in print or online,
that serve me well.
I've just never felt an urge
to drink anything with
notes of crushed rock
or undertones of forest floor.
I'd rather not blend licorice
with lavender or lead pencil
at any point of fermentation.
Cherries and berries are okay,
but why add tobacco or espresso
to the bouquet?
I simply don't care if a wine is
sexy or kinky,
opulent or flamboyant;
and I'm certainly not interested
in knowing whether or not
it has good drainage
and a long finish.
Frankly, I'm afraid of a vintage
that's too exuberant,
full-bodied, and penetrating,
especially if it shows some
secondary characteristics from bottle age.
Do the people who write
such rhetoric really expect me
to take them seriously?
If so, they have clearly imbibed

so many fruits of the vine
that their brains have become
vats of verbiage
left on the lees too long.

Carol Steinhagen

The Days of the Week

An orange cat in black vest cavorts
on a purple swing. Light blue streaks
trace his back and forth, forth and back.
Green dashes under the paws are grass.

This is the Sunday cat, an apostate
who fritters away free time. The weekday cats
get down to business: washing on Monday,
ironing on Tuesday .... They count her days as,

after milking and doing dishes, she compels
her knotted fingers to draw the needle
through flimsy dishtowel cotton
along the pattern's blue lines.

In and out, out and in
she pulls the threads to bring
these little compliant creatures to life
in any color she chooses. The red iron

of Tuesday's yellow cat doesn't sear.
Friday's golden pie doesn't turn black
in the oven. An efficient purple cat
holds it over her green apron like a prize

no man would devour in silence.
Saturday's pink shopping cats carry
little black purses fat with coins.
Blue streaks under their paws mark their pace.

Tilting the cheese-spread glass,
she takes a sip of his JD. Just
an inch she poured, enough to finish
the swing's purple ropes before she hears
the thud of his boots in the kitchen.

Rikki Santer

Menu

Tall tri-fold opens
        like a French door

the sketchbook of your appetite clutches
its crotch   you could eat this way

forever in glossy foreplay   all major
credit cards willing   hunted heads

fill with rum hum on sweet feedback
loops   light or dark eruptions stir

the spines of all Suffering Bastards   no
checks please   liquor your currency

     the careless lipstick of your waitress
last night's Zombie goop still in her curls

her sword's flame unfurls your flank
steak   onto your plate   right next to that next

butt of Lucky Strike   last course Big Fat
Mamasan's dry ice breath swallows whole

two hairless dogs of a cleavaged patron
     their rhinestone leashes dangle like tongues

from Big Fat's creamy lower lip
       dessert has dessert.

Lana Hechtman Ayers

Red Riding Hood Remembers Grandma
Grief is a circular staircase.
—Linda Pastan

She's dead and buried now
and can't speak for herself.
So I'll never really know how she felt
about my romance with the Wolf.

But Grandma believed in taking a chance,
always making bus trips to Atlantic City
to "tickle" the one-armed bandits.
She was the queen of early bird

dinners at the diner and had a healthy
slosh of brandy before noon.
The best advice she ever gave me
was to do whatever it was I wanted

as long as it didn't land me in jail
(though if it did, call her, she'd make bail).
"Because, Red," she said, "life is
a single shot of malt liquor, last call,

so drink up and have a ball."
And the Wolf, who shared more than a few
brews with her at Hans Andersen's Tavern,
called her "a chewy old bone,"

meaning it as a compliment.
When Grandma passed away, everyone,
even Baba Yaga, showed up at the pub
to lift a mug of lager in her honor.

Koon Woon

Brooding

Emily Dickinson "tasted a liquor never brew'd,"
And Shakespeare had tamed the shrew.
But if I don't find a bottle of wine fast,
I will be screwed.

I have been brooding over the "midnight lore."
I found in my scribblings but there's more
Words I meant to say that are in deep mud,
Like bovine creatures eat the grass they cud.

So I go to the Century Tavern in the U-District,
Where the philosophy students hang out,
To play pinball on a machine named "King Cool,"
And wouldn't you know it, I scored the highest
Of the brightest, but that was in the previous century,
When the Kingdome was imploded to build
CenturyLink Field.

And of all places, there is now a pinball museum
In Seattle Chinatown, in spite of all digital games
With lifelike avatars, the theory of ideas marches on.
But at the pinball museum the goal still is
To get your balls on top and make the game last,
And until the balls get flipped out and fall into the gutter,
Man, you are still "King Cool."

Steve Wilson

Little Poem for Edward Gorey

Something mutters at the trim
of the page—a word or two
concealed within an heiress's coat.

At the gallery opening, she draws them
to herself again, under her breathing,
beside a dimmed canvas. It is raining now

across the broad plains of Kenya, where
syllables range, sweat, conspire
to become: the needle within her thoughts—

at once certain and sheltered. What is
this sound—sound's shape? The voice of
a lover leaving? What trails through air

remorseless as this slender glass of Sémillon,
abandoned beside a paisley chair?
Speak. Speak, pale form, lest I be lost.

Laurence Snydal

Peasant Dance
after Bruegel's painting

See them dancing in the square
Over here.
Is it just the country air
Or the beer?
Watch the piper squeeze the skin,
Mouthpiece drooping on his chin,
Where the music must begin
To appear.

His companion sports a plume
In his hat.
Offers ale that we assume
Will be flat.
Close behind him village sots
Swigging from their earthen pots
Sing with tuneless roars the thoughts
Of the vat.

Ardent as his hat the lover
Busses his beloved maid.
In the background we discover
Town and people all displayed.

Hand in hand the farmers prance
Scrape and bow.
Harlequin salutes the dance,
Shows them how.
From the inn the bar wench drawn.
Children practice on the lawn.
Malt and music carry on,
Then as now.

Ragg Mopp

walk and you walk, turn and you turn; but try to walk
or turn and you're suddenly worried about where your
arms are, which way your face is facing. Alice tells me
I shouldn't hate our dance coach, Hector. I said I don't
hate anybody—but I hate Hector. He's a scapegoat for
feeling like a toddler, plus I hate how he counts "one
two three four and turn and turn and through." What
kind of grammar is that? It throws me off, and that's
his fault. But because this whole swing thing came out
of Alice's impeccable head, I muddle through, counting
and walking and turning two three four in this new and
throwback, natural and hectored way, but at least there's
good, old music. And at last, Hector ushers us to the ball
where there's a live band and people who have been at
this for a while. We do our four moves, and we do them
again. And again. And then we have a couple of beers,
Alice and I. And then we take to the dance floor with
lead and follow and turn and through gone right down
the coal chute because the best dance coach is beer.

James Rodgers

You Know You Like Beer

You know you like beer
when you ask for a sample
of a beer
you've tried before
just to get
an extra free three ounces.
You know you like beer
when you name your cats
Hops and Barley.
You know you like beer
when you've already researched
the brewpubs
of a new city you're visiting,
and base your hotel
on its proximity to beer.
You know you like beer
when specialty bottles
take up the entire bottom shelf
of your refrigerator.
You know you like beer
when you plan your dinner menu
based on the beers
in your refrigerator.
You know you like beer
if you're drinking one
while reading this poem.
You know you like beer
if you brew your own.
You know you like beer
if you join a club
that goes and drinks beer

just so you don't drink alone,
and have an excuse
to drink more beer.
You know you like beer
if you have any taste at all.

Jerry Vaughn

A Spam Good Idea

"Would you like a can of beer?"
"Yes, I would. If one is near."
"But do you know, and did you hear
That Spam goes good with lots of beer?"

"You're saying Spam is good with beer?"
"Yes, I am. I hope that's clear!
And if you try it you won't jeer.
Instead you'll pause and give a cheer."

"So, will you share some Spam with me?
Especially if the beer is free?"
"I will my friend for Spam is great.
And in a sandwich, it is first rate.
But only with a beer to drink.
They go together. That's what I think!"

"Now let us sit and share a dinner
For drinking beer makes Spam a winner.
And when I dish this Spam for you
Let us share a can or two."

Robert Perchan

Gastronomy of Seduction

I like my tomatoes totally stewed.
—Locker room vulgarity

I like my steaks juicy and fully nude.
My salads sassy and my veggies crude.
My beer street-wise and St. Pauli brewed.
My potato jacketed but slit-open lewd.
My wine slyly coy—neither slut nor prude.
My dessert provocative—even tabooed.
The trick is getting my food in the mood.

Beer and Fish

Piaute Red, Bullhead Bronze, Old Bluegill,
Pumpkinseed Seasonal Ale, Fast Bass Malt,

Stout Trout Stout, Walleye Rye, Crappie Lager,
Pan-fish Pale, Sea Run Porter, Irish Salmon Slough,

Whitefish Whit, Poindexter Brown, Sierra
Red Band Amber, Husky Musky I.P.A.

Five Grain Minnow Mush, Fourteen Mile Reach,
Three Eyed Perch, Two Year Draught, Hanford
Steelhead.

Lahontan Light, Bitchy Brook Brew, Low River Red,
Irrigation Ditch Dark, Heavy Sediment Stout,

Trashfish Tailout, Roundtail Relief, Razorback Rough,
Native Nail Biter, Non-Native Bite Nail-er, Poach n'

High Tailer, Yeast n' Dregs, Ham n' Pegs, Didymo
Draft, Whirling Disease Wheat, Mud Snail Slap,

Heavy Metal Headwaters, Troubled Tributaries,
Tricky Squawfish, Stalling Senators, Spectacular

Spectators, Quench Not Staunch, Save Salmon,
Save Steelhead, Save Rivers and Streams.

Flavor Savors Last Sip. Slip Slop. Fish More,
Catch More, Release More. Then Enjoy Your Beer.

Thomas Lequin

Beer Store and Beer People

I sit at the vegetable stand across the road.
Truck and car after truck and car pull in.
Never a quiet moment at the beer store.

I've been told the beer store sells 450 packs each week,
Miller, Coors, Bud, Piels, Schlitz, Old Milwaukee,
Narragansett, and even John Adams.

It comes out the door, carried by beer people,
three steps down.
The blonde, pony-tailed, a six-pack for each hand.
Guy, bearded, belly protruding, a twelve-pack.
Angry-faced and talking to himself, a Bud man.
A couple, already beered from their morning visit,
back again to fill the late afternoon.

Yes, they sell other things.
A man once came out carrying a gallon of milk.
The state police came and arrested him for
disorderly conduct.
Beer people can be a tough crowd.

The polka, song and dance:
"In heaven there is no beer,
that's why we drink it here.
And when we're gone from here,
all our friends will be drinking all the beer."

Beer people know this.
There is no time to waste.

Jared Leising

The Beer Ted Kooser Owes Us All

Twenty-four hours in a day, 24 beers in a case.
Coincidence? I think not.
—H.L. Menken

I go to Safeway
to buy a six-pack.
Somebody's taken
a bottle from the
last pack, so now it's

a fiver, dammit.
Was it Kooser? —that
geezer (my mom finds
cute) who wrote about
the miracle of

a lone beer bottle
standing right side up
and empty along
the highway—each line
three syllables long,

each stanza three lines.
My students read this
without awe, as though
they've done this plenty
after polishing

off a bottle at
fifty, cruising down
Aurora, tossing
emptiness to wind.

II. Belly Up to the Bar

Barbara Lydecker Crane

Finding Rumi in a Wine Bar
in the ancient Persian form of a ghazal

With wine to whet his lips, Rumi's words do not run out.
He says, "Loosen your tongue–don't worry what comes out."

He wiggles fingers in the air. "Don't hand me another glass.
Just pour it in my mouth." Rumi guzzles, then hums out,

"Having nothing produces provisions." If only he'd give me
a hint of how to net a harvest when the tide of income's out.

He tells of emptiness, patience, and whirling as one waits:
"Dance, when broken open." At that a gentle lute strums out.

"Sufism is the feeling of joy when disappointment comes."
I ask him, do Sufis never sulk? Do they decree glum out?

Rumi tells a tale of a Sufi's joy eclipsing dismay. "Prophet
Muhammad lost a boot. Of course he was bummed out

when an eagle swooped, plucked it up, and off it flew.
That boot turned upside-down, and what tumbled out?

A poisonous snake! God sends us disappointment to elude
disaster. So sing, Barb, and bring the flute and drums out."

Rumi's words, in quotes (which I have paraphrased in
places) are from *The Essential Rumi*, translations by
Coleman Barks with John Moyne.

Gail Tyson

Old-Time Round

This deck's a drumskin beneath Maggie's tail,
her ear cocked to the sweet harmonica moan
of sap rising, phlox and bare-root iris
fiddling in the rock garden, love cresting

in our tones. She hears the ramps plucking
at the flinty soil, lichen piping on the brook
and sapphires deep down, dark as bass notes.
Nose twitching to a highland beat, she keeps time

with her ancestral pack, while butterflies
tremble like mandolins and rain quickens,
turning our tin roof into a snare drum,
the rhythm of belonging in this place.

Tonight the boys will be pickin' to the score
of stars, white notes on a sable pelt so wide,
and sipping Scottish communion
until the moon slips sideways. For now

ballads are bridging from pines to maples,
the gravel road curling, curling.

Susan J. Erickson

Self-Portrait as a Secret

I am the loose floorboard stepped over
even in the dark. I am tight lips sailing a ship
through enemy waters. I am the hangnail
never trimmed with cuticle scissors.

I am the mole at the base of the neck
disguised with flesh-colored makeup.
Late at night Google "skin transplants." Nothing
is ever deleted from the hard drive. Nothing.

I am the squatter who pays no rent but demands
a guard dog at each door and windows blinded
by blackout shades. I am a virus replicating
in each cell. It will take surgery
and a round of radiation to remove me.

Sometimes after a fourth mojito at Havana Street Bar
I drop hints to my identity. Then the bartender
announces the cab is at the curb
and collects the tab for the evening.

If cross-examined I slouch in the witness chair,
plead the Fifth. Not everyone remembers
the color of their eyes.

Tiffany L. Thomas

The Sleeping Saints' Sapphic Test Case

We are watching the Jackson Square psychics at work
| when | my throbbing, fresh-stitched hand sends glass
and gin and lime into your lap | then | St. Hildegard,
drowsing warm in the pagan sweat between my
breasts, opens one sterling eye, but there is nothing
| given | except my gimlet-dipped fingers curing in the
half high sun.

Gretchen Fletcher

Fear of the Dark

When evening fell upon the island
and the day held on as if with claws,
gasping a last breath reluctant to give in
and admit its death, we wandered off

the tourist-traveled streets and made our way
into dark markets where rats ran
and local boys dusky as night
approached with threats unspoken.

In the lack of light, fear
clamped down as with a moray's jaws
and held us paralyzed. But at midnight
by the white light of hotel lamps

we laughed at fear
over lime-sliced gin and tonics,
and the click plink of ice cubes
against the sides of glasses.

Carla Shafer

Boutique Brewery

Call it bird song if you want
but it is "brew song" bright and sharp,
bitter and sweet, bubbles floating across
the tongue. Liquid, like the trill of a robin,
interspersed with the plaintive screech
of a seagull or listen for the keening
whistle of the red-tailed hawk before it
dives to the counter where shoulder-rubbing
stool-perchers twitter and tweet
on tap flavors sipped through afternoon
and into the night. Broad hands rest
on a neighbor's arm or haunch, all
friendly-like, no regard for personal space,
like quarter notes sung in an easy range.
From here, a twelve-hour drive.
Look for me around eight.

Jeff Walt

Becoming a Regular

Your face is the first thing they'll remember,
then odd habits like clanking your glass
with an index finger, dashing salt
into your beer, or staring
deep into the murk

of the mirror behind the bar. They'll memorize
your drink and bless you
with a moniker in honor of the cocktail you love
best—JD or Wild Duck or Ms. Scotch-on-the-rocks until
the bartender introduces you to the regulars. Someone

will offer you a light or bum a cigarette, move
from his usual stool and tell you about his life,
the wrecked marriage, how
his kids won't talk to him and no one
gives a shit, really,

not even his parole officer. They'll expect
to hear the details of your bad luck: How old
were you when your old man split?
When'd you take your first hit? Who
got the kids? They'll ask where

you're from and wonder what twist of fate
gave you permission to sit at The Finish Line
all day. Then, while standing in the shower
or sitting on the toilet, you'll suddenly think about them,
wonder where they live, what the house looks like, how

did your lives end up crashed
and piled in the salvage yard of a bar?
Some days they'll listen to your problems.
Some days they'll tell you to get lost.
They'll buy you lemon-drop shots and share

warm cashews. Together you'll scratch instant
Lotto tickets, beg God to plop a million
in your pockets, watch *The Price Is Right*, complain
out loud when your contestant doesn't win.
When you don't show up for days, the rest

will begin to imagine what's wrong, ponder
calling the police. And when you return,
several call your name as you walk through
the door, that thin, trembling spine of light follows
right behind you. They'll raise a hand or beer

to toast your arrival: this is how you'll know
how much they love you;
this is how you'll know how much.

Victory Park

When my tenth-grade history teacher said
instead of combat, I could *entertain the troops,*
my fists clenched. These days I open
my hands to find a pen, a spray of basil.

Evan pours Remy Martin into a snifter, unsnaps
his silver Zippo, twirls the glass over the flame.
I want to serve up crème brulée, flourish of berry,
drizzle of syrup, thin layers of bittersweet shrapnel.

Evan grabs my ass, chain-smokes, trash-talks
his ex-boyfriend, sings along to jukebox Billie Holiday—
It's nobody's business, if I do.
What can we muster on behalf of belief?

Across the street Nick the Barber is turning 70.
En El Mexicano Sarita serves
complimentary goat to the regulars.
A thin man limps through Victory Park.

Avra Kouffman

The Frozen Zone

We had some good times together.
As a team, we made people laugh.
With you, the evenings rolled along—
a happy mix of predictable and not-so.

Variations on a theme:
less a question of where we'd go
than how far we'd go.

If I stopped at our old haunts now,
I'd expect to find you there
and that is why I rarely do.
Instead, I seek out places I won't see you.

It was hard on our friends.
They didn't want us to part.
But faced with a choice,
they chose you.

I cared for my friends.
How many more will I lose?
Now that I've gone off you,
my madcap ex-love, booze.

Paul Hostovsky

The Debate at Duffy's

She said that sex was a yearning of the soul.
He said it was a very compelling argument
of the body, a compulsion. She said it was
a spiritual compulsion. He said it was nothing
if not carnal, *carni*, meat. This conversation
took place in a bar. The background music was
so loud it was in the foreground. The bodies
on the dance floor were moving in ways that
would interest even the dead if they could only
remember how to live. There was a baseball game
playing on television. On the table were two
empty glasses and the bottle's green phallus
which she took in her hand and pulled toward her,
pulling him toward her as she poured them both
another drink. He drank deeply, felt the spirit
filling his cup. Then he looked into her eyes and saw
that she was beautiful, sexy, and at the bottom
of the 9th, suddenly, surprisingly, irrevocably, right.

Brenna Lemieux

Five-oh-one

It starts in the spring, via email.
Time in the subject line, bar in the body.
Simple. They stay for a drink, maybe two.
Then two at least. The light dawdles, the air
thaws. Five-oh-one? They ask, or sometimes,
Six-oh-one?, when a meeting runs long.
Three of them, to be clear: him and him and her.
Sometimes his wife. Him and his wife and him
and her. They're seeing a show tonight,
they must leave at seven. But he's just ordered
one more, so she does too, waving to the spouses.
A pattern, you might say: light stretched thinner,
longer in the sky, drinks blurring her like
a flow tide, train ride home fuzzed and glorious,
his texts buoying her north, her limbs warm
and fluid as she chops her late meal. This
is how we sustain ourselves at work,
we the open-plan drones, the lackeys
in the hands of a tired boss. The keen
arterial leap when his email pops:
Five-oh-one? The pulse trill as she counts six
minutes before she replies. Yes, always yes.
But days can only stretch so far before
they snap back. He and his wife are moving home,
they say one night, holding hands. When the day
comes, he and she—the others—sneak from the office,
pack snacks for the road. Make a card. Send them off.
After that, a long weekend. Drinks.
He mentions, offhand, his girlfriend's trip
to Italy. Girlfriend. Her hard-drive-crashing
heart a Mayday, spiral, a wild off-the-cliff skid.

She smiles and swallows her drink. Slips home, sips
whiskey for dinner, skids down the wall
in a puddle of pond-still misery. Sleeps it off.
Shops and cleans and cooks for the week. Shows up
Monday at eight, bright and brutal, coffee-fueled,
keyboard miles below her skillful, ungrasped palms.

Roger Pfingston

Grady's Imperial Pint

Grady was sitting in the Uptown drinking an imperial
pint of Boddingtons ale with his seafood gumbo when
his wife said she'd changed her mind, instead of lemon
water she thought she'd like an imperial pint, too. It
looks good, she said.

Grady was surprised and even a tiny bit put off. The
imperial pint had always been his drink at the Uptown
while his wife usually favored white wine, a pinot grigio
or lacking that, a chardonnay. At other times, today
for example, she simply asked for water. Suddenly she
wants an imperial pint!

It's a lot of beer, Grady said, hoping the quantity might
give her pause. You're used to a short glass at home,
half a bottle...six ounces! Are you sure? It might not be
the company your eggplant Parmesan expects.

Grady's wife stared in silence across the table, long
enough to make Grady look down at his gumbo and
reconsider his argument. Why in god's name would the
imperial pint be any less complementary to eggplant
Parmesan than it would to your seafood gumbo? she
asked. Grady—and here she leaned forward to whisper
across the table—what the hell's wrong with you!

Rosy Night

We took to Kir Royales in Quebec
near the waterfront, under our *lune de miel.*
That deep blackcurrent red—we sipped

the sweet effervescent blood of the field
as summer dusk pinked the tablecloth
in that bistro down the cobblestone hill.

Wasn't it Le Médaillon? It was more than
thirty years ago. So it might be
I recall the medallions of veal.

I haven't thought of it till now
at this bar I poke into after everything
else is over and I'm still downtown,

not ready to ferry myself home
and enter alone. Here I can watch
the tiny white bulbs strung to the shelves,

the lights like near stars, and the bottles
dumb local gods who've followed
my troubles. Where's your heart wandered

old lover, mother of our grown young?
Why not another cassis and prosecco—
a rosy night over the river.

Sneha Subramanian Kanta

Aftertaste

wine harmonizes in an arrant glass:
shaped by amorphous sand granules
that deliquesce to conceive crystalline.

post meridian, aqueous yellow-gray skies
record simulacrums. nighttime, a cloistered
canary neon bulb imbibes inertia.

ante meridiem, vivid escapades perch
leftover wisps of a bare glass;

where it felt as though i touched your lips,
in those bygone, dark hours.

Nancy Nowak

War Effort

The burnt umber bar
though nicked and scarred
is burnished to a gloss
almost viscous, as if something dark
had been spilled across its grain.

She's just off the day shift at Republic
inspecting the wings of P-47 Thunderbolts

with the usual Friday
gang, Doris, Helene, first rounds
served on Rheingold coasters when

soldiers from Camp Upton, after checking
through the tavern window, join them.

They're new recruits, marooned
in the Pine Barrens a few weeks
before being shipped off, some distant
fort or field   no one knows

who have found this oasis
somewhere between Patchogue and Port Jeff
just as the Wurlitzer begins to play
Bésame Mucho: *Each time I cling to your kiss
I hear music divine*. One of them
sweeps her off the barstool; she hesitates, thinks

no, her cousin Evvie could, who wins
jitterbug contests at the Paramount; even so
it's all in fun, everyone laughing
as they dip and swirl, and he's

not serious, though the song
could tear a heart out with longing
as it throbs.

And he's *good*, so for an instant
they both are
lifted above the world
war, unaware.

Elizabeth Shiller

The Boxcar Lounge

Sitting here a while
And I already feel like kissing
Your whiskey lips.
My only issue,
I still taste the coherent air.

But I'll give you a go.
Order me up some, honey
I'm ready for anything.
Give me tonight
To go against what I know.

Douglas M. Smith

Chicago Girl

tulip stemmed wrists
  cigarette fingers
broken nails
   painted yellow
not bitten
hastily clipped
down to the stubs

the backs
  of her hands
creamy smooth
underneath
dry and callused

late summer
  intentionally lost
    in
Wisconsin woods
somewhere near Wausau
   she holds
a glass of white wine
to her lips
  but does not open
her mouth

she sits atop
a long smooth boulder
  in the middle
of a narrow rapids
  daydreaming
dips her feet
into the shallow river

         sighs and lowers
the glass
onto a rock

"You don't like
the wine?" he asks.

The wind catches her
long black hair
and whips
around her
pale white face
         he can't see
her eyes
         only
that tight
chapped
disappointed smile

Rooftop Bar in June Haze

No sky tonight, and we strangers
up from the street won't find it
where we drink in this stonework-
and-brick paved garden. I lift

my whiskey higher, tumbler tilted
to a nightful of fog, to you my lost
lovers and early sweethearts, as if
you hover here in the mist. I do

feel the soothe, moist and cool
on my brow—a gesture? Could be
the damp air does harbor our echoes,

our after-pleasures, and your vapor
grazes this glass I raise, to you,
who taught me to be tender.

David Lloyd

Tafarn Dwynant
Ceinws, Wales

The boys are draining Carlings as they bank
and shave and plunk:

Shortie, Spedog, JesusSpider, fist-bumping,
high-fiving.

And why not? —with "Higher Ground" blasting
and megaliths still hoisting

capstones, the women and children evacuated;
the past littered

in corners; the future in the alley bin.
Carry on boys. There's no sin

in lingering.
The world might be limping

towards fire and ice,
but here the space-time vortex

stalls
as the cueball falls

across freshly-brushed green.

John Morgan

Ambush

A light with the richness
of cream pours over the bar.
Slack night. I sip a glass
of beer remembering who I think
I am and then forgetting.
"Killing's more direct than talk,"

he says, says he could do it still
but what's the use? His breath's
a heavy metal stink about like dirt
or the wide circles
of waiting he pledged allegiance to
before his birth.

Camped in the Asian,
dark, sick on his first patrol,
he tells me how they wouldn't
talk to him, his alien platoon
that first night out. Then
something like a finger beckoning.

He turns, hears in his middle ear
a bird's frail tune,
thick eons shouldering over oceans of recall.
With hardly time to think
he's off his stool, rolling
in a fit of peanut shells and drool.

The mind at war
has got its reasons. Plunging
in a sink of need,
he's there as well as here
hands tensed around his snub-nosed,
sharp-toothed pet,

and suddenly I could do
with one less beer. Tomorrow
if he lives he'll
burn a village, be a vet.
All wars are fought by country
boys used to this long road.

Oblivion

Our trio departed Youngstown,
Vonnegut's *Time Quake* on cassettes,
past scattered remnants
of canal along the interstate
to Rochester and revelry.

Ultimatums expired
as told by politicians
and retired generals
blitzing from televisions
disarming the homefront.

Too old to draft, we named
the drink "Shock and Awe"
to commemorate the invasion.
We discussed it too casually,
victims of the blitz.

Inverted fireworks and spectacle
narrated by excited anchors hiding
behind fake stoicism and branding.
Maneuvering death and explosions
into their own ignoble image.

The "Bunker Buster" was assembled;
a coalition of the available.
Whiskeys of America and Britain
dropped into a patriotic brew
To all go down together.

Combat reporters embedded,
reserves supporting the home front,
strategically deploying information,
igniting fear and speculation,
thickening the fog-of-war.

Fearing the blowback inherent
with bad decisions and whiskey,
we made our exit strategies:
the bathroom, the sink, the patio shrubs,
then charged into friendship lore.

Long Creek, Walla Walla

We'd be drinking at a bar in La Grande on a Saturday
   night,
a few of us from the Duncan section,
when all of a sudden
somebody'd say, "Let's go to Long Creek!"

So we'd pile into the back of his pickup
and drive for hours
through the vast, sagebrush-scented eastern Oregon
   night
till we came to a cluster of buildings—a tavern
at a crossroads
in the middle of nowhere.

Not a whole lot was happening
in the Long Creek tavern (which later I learned
was called by the locals a "pastime").
Juke box silent.
Pool table deserted.
One lone cowboy and the barmaid
palavering...

I was trying to figure
why we had come there and what it all meant.
I was new to the West, and distances
were improbable.

. . . . .

Well, who knows what it meant, and who knows
where it was we went
from there.
	Back to work on Monday morning
tamping ballast, lining track,
maintaining the twenty miles of Union Pacific roadbed
known as "the Duncan section."

Other weekends it'd be different.
We'd be drinking at a bar in Pendleton
and suddenly
somebody'd say, "Let's go to Walla Walla!"

Mott Creek Spike Camp

I was a line worker fighting forest fires when I turned twenty-two. It was 1970, Okanagon-Wenatchee National Forest, Mott Creek Spike Camp. I was on a tiny crew, just three of us: my friend Chip and me, and Bill Moody, the roughneck crew leader, a tough giant from Butte, Montana, who was fresh out of jail.

We wanted to celebrate my birthday, but we were fifty miles from anywhere; the only vehicle was the Forest Service pickup. Bill borrowed it, so we piled in and drove two hours to the nearest bar.

We didn't have a lot of money, but when the good citizens (or at least the ones who were at the Entiat Tavern that night) found out we were firefighters and it was my birthday, they bought us round after round. Other firefighters had saved that town, after all. There was much backslapping and thanks and too much alcohol. When the tavern closed, Bill passed out, so we hoisted his huge body into the bed of the pickup and headed back. I don't remember who drove the pickup.

When we got back two forest rangers were waiting with the sheriff, and they were not happy. Turns out Bill had been refused permission when he asked to borrow that Forest Service pickup. They were going to arrest us, but Chip and I protested our ignorance, and Bill only came awake enough to vomit. They decided not to press charges when they found out it was my birthday. But the real reason they let us off was we were good at putting out fires too small to send a full crew after. I don't remember how we got Bill to his tent.

Next day we were in bad shape. We tried telling them we were sick, but that didn't fly. They sent us out anyway, on a tough four-mile hike down a rugged mountain from where the chopper dropped us. We put out a smoldering stump, a job that had to be done to prevent it from starting a blowup fire, like the ones the twelve-man crews got. The helicopters didn't fly after dark, and it was all we could do to get back in time, and not be stranded for the night on that mountain. That's all I remember. Hey, I was still drunk.

Robert Michael Pyle

Duffy's Deck: 27 July 2015

Yellow-striped jumping spider leaps to my knee.
Steller's jay vaults the river, which loops
around the gravel bar under alders and elms,
ninebark and knotweed, then slingshots
down to the bay, on this 90-degree afternoon.
Wait till winter! When the river roars through here,
almost up to the deck, and I take my pint inside,
into dim orange light and endless Irish tapes.

But for now,
out here on Duffy's deck, with the crows,
the mergansers, the jays, as the day drops
through 80, to 70, and more,
perfection seems possible.

Yet still my pint runs out.

Al Fresco

Tranquility? Not yet. Cheap chardonnay,
chips, guacamole must suffice. I drink
outside, preferring traffic over guys who play
dice games or darts or wobbly pool. I think
the operation's underway. You're out
for hours beneath bright lights, beneath slim tools
in steady hands. I'm here to smother doubt—
a Redwood City dive, my ship of fools.
I am no captain, just a stowaway.
I probably should find that room designed
for meditation, and I probably should pray,
beseech a stained glass God, but I'm inclined
to order one more round and study license plates
on passing cars. Close by, your surgeon concentrates.

Bird Watch

competitive nests hum after 8 pm—
feathered creatures flock to bars
along second avenue.

peacocks in suits
clink beer bottles,
sing karaoke off-key.

peafowl in raised hemlines
play sexual pantomime.

robins and canaries
wing it with penguin bartenders
and flamingos sashay
to the disco beat.

the night brings them in—
those sugar daddy owls
and fast-talking hummingbirds
and gossipmonger parrots.

pigeons outnumber the exotics
and too many chickens and turkeys
make the scene foul.

in the corner,
a sparrow sips her merlot,
thinks about scrambled eggs
and flying solo.

the wine gives her courage,
but her wings are too stiff
to make the move.

David Alpaugh

Last Call

Cedar waxwings really get it.
They know it's better to give than receive.
They also know an hour or so of wine tasting
goes a long way toward boosting conviviality.
(They are the bon *vivants* of birdland.)

Lining up on the branch of a pyracantha
or cherry tree, they pass half-fermented fruit
up & down the bar—till most of them are blotto.

Every avian once-in-a-while,
a waxwing who's had ten too many
leaves the pub without a designated pilot
—stumbling off into the sky—
and, blood alcohol way too high,
flies into air that will not yield.

Hearing that dull, disheartening thud,
I've wiped blood from my patio window
and buried a drunken *Bombycilla cedrorum*
twice this winter (pretty necks broken).

Unlike thousands of wingless DUIs,
who whizz through red lights and stop signs,
they never kill anyone but themselves.

Steve Hood

Bootleg

It happened on Valentine's Day,
when Capone wanted to get rid of Bugs
and his gang in north Chicago.

Saint Valentine secretly married
Christian couples against Roman law,
and for that he was executed.

Wearing police uniforms, they
shot with Tommy guns seven
men lined up facing a brick wall.

Every year millions of the smitten
bring wine to their sweet lovers,
pierced by arrows of desire,

like the men in suits, ties, fedoras,
dressed for dates on the town,
who kissed their lives goodbye.

Rena Priest

The Hobo and His Pigeons

The sound-the-sound of longing in the streets,
Ti-tum-ti-tum-ti-tum-ti-tum-ti-tum.
My chum's a bum for rum who lives in slums.
He craves the meat of beasts with beets and leeks,
and sings his longing to the burdened beaks
of birds who sing, "I want, I want, ti-tum."
Those burdened beaks, they long and sing for crumb
from bum with rum and roses in his cheeks.

And when he speaks he coos them out a jest
of bars and men and broads and roads he's known
to give them ease of heavy hungry loads
and fill their beaks with sweetened emptiness
while he forgets the bleary blurry cold
in songs of longing and remembrances.

Jerry Bradley

If You're Drinking to Forget, Please Pay in Advance

Priests in plain clothes, insomniacs afraid to close their
    eyes,
refugees from the sleep club with vacant stools on
    either side,
parolees, defrocked veterans, women wearing little
    more than a nightie,
encrusted vomit in a bathroom even a MerryMaid
    couldn't keep tidy,
thermoses of hot coffee, beer nuts, and happy hour
    pizzas,
rascals on the run whispering endearments to
    señoritas,
first timers drinking with bikers at the bar, soldiers
    home on leave,
forlorn housewives escaping the kitchen table and
    looking for a place to grieve
where the barmaid goes to the well for another vodka
    and schnapps,
licks her sticky lips and primes the tip jar, putting two
    fives on top,
smiles at out-of-towners, blowhards, eavesdroppers
    making dirty calls
beneath Christmas decorations months out of season,
    the sounds of losers racking balls
and all their idle threats, swearing next time to really
    kick the ass
of the guardian angel on the shoulder of the smirking
    guy refilling his glass.

Jennifer Bullis

Incompetent Mixologist

The one with alternating layers
of Bailey's and Kahlua
and a squeeze of lemon on top
is it Melting Tundra
yeah no that's a Crabby Tabby

Melting Tundra is one part carbon
and three parts hydrogen
wait no it's ice and Bailey's
and peanut butter frappéd
with a spiral of ranch dressing on top

or the one with the methylated stress gene
I think that's anise and vodka
blended with ice and early trauma
served in a glass slipper
yeah that's an Epigenetics

hold on Epigenetics is
three fingers of gin
two fingers parental neglect and
one finger punitive religion or is that
Substitutionary Atonement

wait no Substitutionary Atonement is gin
cranberry bitters and muddled grief
served room temperature
in a hand-hewn wooden mug
with a two-part chaser

first they make you drink
a pewter tankard of juniper-berry juice
unfermented
and second they make you
confront your parents and your worst date

or is it the Meet-Cute no that's
the one where you pour a thimbleful of champagne
and a jigger of triple-milled over
a dropped dollar bill and you both kneel down
and lick it off the floor

Shirley J. Brewer

Goddess of Swizzle

Two stirring weeks
at the Maryland Bartending Academy
earn me an MBA. A perfect score
tops off my final test—concocting
twenty drinks in less than ten minutes.
The huge clock behind the bar
keeps time with swizzle sticks.

Drunk with success, I find
a job at a waterfront dive
called Captain Clyde's. Late in the day,
men saunter in from skipjacks,
plop down on stools, order lemonade pie
and beer. Beer! The Goddess of Mixology
pours suds into deep blue steins.

I long for an occasion to slice limes
into neat wedges, pluck
a maraschino cherry from its ruby cage.
Past sunset, aquamarine lights
glow in the mammoth jukebox.
Couples dance on dark brown carpet
that bunches up like walrus hide.

Mellow with hops, the oystermen
sing their chanteys. Even the moon
tunes in—a gleaming white coaster.
I forget about Manhattans,
Pomegranate Martinis, Side Cars.
Stars like specks of beer foam
spatter the perfect night sky.

Lucy Tyrrell

Margarita

Midori, the barista,
measures and pours
tequila into the stainless canister
with smooth moves
like dancing.
She steps forward when she
measures and pours
agave nectar and orange liqueur.
She presses the half lime
with both hands—she's
clapping without sound.
She lids ice and liquids
and shakes with rhythm
of castanets.
She sways as she wets
the glass rim with a piece of lime
and rolls it in salt.
Her bare elbow lifts as she
pours the chilled drink
over new ice cubes
in the glass.
She adds a wheel of lime
and turns with a smile
to place the margarita
on the counter next
to my platter of enchiladas
with red chile sauce.
I haven't tasted this
drink yet, but I
want another, just so I can
watch her dance again.

Susan Mahan

Last Night in Paris

I enter a café that looks out on Notre Dame Cathedral.
I sit near the window and
order a glass of beaujolais wine.
I have learned to love beaujolais on this trip.
I wonder if beaujolais means good and beautiful?
I'll have to find out.
I write the word in my journal.

I'm looking at the bread on the table next to me.
I love bread and have eaten it with every single meal
for the past ten days.
I'd like to distract that couple and grab a piece.
There seem to be fewer social restraints in Paris,
but I don't think I can get away with *that*.

When I leave the café, I see a guy I met a few nights ago.
He asks me to go back in and have a cup
of coffee with him.
Pourquoi pas?
We talk about the club where I read a few poems
and about my disillusionment
with what I saw of the french poetry scene.
I tell him I am a serious poet and as I say this,
I realize for the first time, that it's true.
I tell him it's my last night in Paris.
He writes his name and address in my journal
and says if I ever come back,
I will already know him, at least.

I am dining at a Greek restaurant.
I came in because the handsome man outside
who looks like Harrison Ford convinces me

that I will like the food.
Sidewalk hawking is part of his job, and it works on me.

I order a demi-bouteille of wine
because the waiter convinces me I should.
I am not usually so easily convinced on either count,
but this is my last night in Paris.
The wine is smooth, the food is delicious,
and the lively music envelops me with
each passing moment and with each swallow of wine.

The bottle is empty, and I am drunk.
I want to dance with Harrison Ford.
I can imagine living on a sun-drenched Greek island
and making love outdoors with ....

The music stops.
I see a dishwasher with decayed teeth smiling at me.
I shudder at the thought that he is reading my journal
or my mind.

The music begins again.
They are playing that Greek wedding song.
I forget the name,
but I know I could dance it if I tried.

It's my last night in Paris,
but the world is full of possibilities,
and I feel beaujolais.

Rick Kempa

I Am Sorry That I Knocked on Your Door to Say "Hi"

It was rude of me to be so friendly
so late in the evening as I walked by your house
on my way home from the bar.

People don't do this kind of thing anymore.
People may have never done this kind of thing.
I just looked up and there was your house,

and the thought of your goodness and grace
washed over me, and I knocked on your door.
I may have wanted to hug you, I don't know.

You stood in the doorway and stared at me.
I said "hi," and you said "hi," and I said, "I just
wanted to say 'hi,'" and you said, "All right,"

and you held the door open wide so that
cold air poured into your kitchen.
You were in your pajamas, and barefoot.

It was then I remembered that your lady
lived there too, and it was then that I thought
oh shit. Suddenly, I felt like who I was—

a goofy old drunk shuffling home in the dark.
"Do you want to come in?" you said at last
(although you still stood in your door).

I did not want to come in. I did not want
to have done what I had just done.
I just wanted to say "hi."

Melissa Grossman

Beer & Tulips

Cast into the dirt beside my house I find
a bouquet of white and purple tulips
and an empty can of beer. Had a jilted lover
tossed the tulips aside and soaked his despair
with malted suds? Or, had the lover
approached his love already soaked?
It saddens me to see such possibility lost.
I lift the limp bundle, wire ribbon
still tied around them in a bow. The tulips
droop in my grasp. Their petals
shimmer in sunlight, a pearly translucence.
Such beauty dispossessed cries to me.
I too, have been thrown in the dirt,
felt thirst for fresh water.

Tamra J. Higgins

At the Pub

So, he says to me, "You told me that,"
and I say, "No, no I didn't. I didn't
know that before now to tell you,"
and he says, "You did know; you told me
that a long time ago before
you forgot it." And I say, "I never knew
it," and take a sip of my half-
pint of Guinness, and he says, "Yes,

yes you did 'cause I remember
you telling me," and I say, "Never
told you before because I never
knew it; I just learned it the other
day, and he says, "Yes, you knew it
'cause the same thing that got you to tell me
this time got you to tell me last time.
I remember," and he wipes the foam
from his upper lip while I say, "No,

I know I didn't know it. If I knew it
I'd remember it," and he says,
"You just don't know you knew it 'cause
you forgot you knew it." And always
the eternal optimist, he adds, "Isn't
it great how we get to know everything
twice now?" And me being the realist
brings him down to earth again
and say, "I know everything

once; it's you who don't know what
you know, so now know everything twice,"
and he says, "What'll the girls think,

us knowing everything once and then
again?" and since I was wondering
the same thing, I say, "I know
they know about how we know
things, but I don't know what
they think about us knowing or not.

It sure is a whole new life for us
to know now, isn't it?" We laugh
and shake our heads, and have another
sip before calling it an early
night and heading home to bed.

John Guzlowski

Talking Drunk to a Drunk Woman
I Don't Know

The party is in another room
but the hallway is safe for silence
and you tell me there is something in winters
that keeps them coming back again and again
and I laugh because I think you said sinners

so again I ask where you come from
and you tell me there are moons
that never see sunlight, books that never
see rain, and I try to shake my head clear

but it doesn't help because you start again:
telling me about the windows in the attic
the basement in your dreams, the cost
of friction when friction means dreaming

I try to stand to go to the bathroom
but you pull me down into a puddle of bones
and finally I know your words make sense.

Richard Parisio

Things to Give Up After Surgery

Start with smoke. Its drifting whorls,
gray skeins of thought or prayer
unspooling skyward, pooling under eaves
like twilight ghosts. The god
that shape-shifts when you reach for him.

Next, wine. Its lilt upon your tongue,
courtesan at all your banquets—
banish her bossa nova dancing.
Douse the campfire she builds
in your chilly heart with water.

As for sex, there are no clear
instructions. Beguiler, smoother, canceller
of all your debts—her candle
smolders at your bedside yet
forbear. Observe the wick's faint glowing.

And now? The one year old
with you knows. He reaches chubby fingers
for a pine's rough bark. That incense
is your genie. You sniff and turn
a bottle filled with light.

Karen Vande Bossche

No Wine Tonight

I'm afraid to drink right now.
Afraid that, instead of a muse,
the wine will become a martyr
to death, to dying, or some
semblance of life lingering.

Usually luring me to write,
to propose wordy pictures,
it might relax the wrong nut
undo a bolt of depression,
an endless washer of woe.

Already I should just sit,
watch a Hallmark movie
and drink hot chocolate;
the happy endings mimicking
someone else's life.

Joan Wiese Johannes

Happy New Year

Just before midnight, we meet in the woods
The snow is so bright we need no flashlights
The stubborn cork will not release the vintage
I suggest you whack the bottle on a tree

The snow is so bright we need no flashlights
"Auld Lang Syne" and still no wine
I suggest you whack the bottle on a tree
You hold high a plastic cup from Kwik Trip

"Auld Lang Syne" and still no wine
We toast to glasses that are always full
You hold high a plastic cup from Kwik Trip
I lift up a goblet from Lucerne

We toast to glasses that are always full
Just before midnight, we meet in the woods
I lift up a goblet from Lucerne
The stubborn cork will not release the vintage

Medieval Consolations

To drink like a Capuchin means drinking poorly.
To drink like a Benedictine means drinking deeply.
Dominicans imbibe pot after pot.
We know Franciscans swill the cellars dry.

God knows how Jesuits drink, says Britt, glass full.
You don't see me quaff, says Tim, glass empty.

I tell you this story:
When I was a young nun we stole red wine
from the altar in the dark of night,
took it to our tiny rooms to sip.
On narrow beds we toasted, laughing hard.
My first, worst wine and best remembered

until that bottle emptied when we met,
for fifty years kept dust free on my shelf.

Kathleen McClung

The Party Guest Considers the Sky
A Cento for Danusha Laméris

Come, let's stand by the window and look out
at night, in the cricket-loud dark,
the sidewalk ahead wet and glistening.
Every language must have a word for this.
Through the dark galaxies of our bodies
we say "wolf" but mean our own hunger,
Houdini underwater, escaping the chained suitcase.
Tell us all the bad things
beauty's made of.

We could have stayed this way
holding a small glass of bourbon,
from the next room
strains of laughter.
As they lift their glasses, make a toast
I want to tell them "don't do it"
except that they reach skyward,
corsages pinned to their breasts,
the slight hum of the banister.

I wish I hadn't said
Patrick's painting looked "ominous."
His breath, steadied, even,
he pretends not to know us.
Doesn't everything that shines carry its own shadow?
Not the language, but the bones
of the language
after our banquet of loss.
Life requires collapse.

140

Step out of your own story,
fragrance of longing, that ache.
Tonight I name you
Switchblade Moon.

Steve Wilson

The Supernumeraries

Offstage, they've seen it all before, the final scene
that calls them from their friendly game of cards.

Someone will be murdered tonight. The count,
foreign-born, sings of a dream: a woman,

alluring behind her green mask, offers wine
to her secret lover. It is a persuasive shade of red.

When he drinks, nightjars scatter for the forest.
It is an omen the count cannot ignore. Who will
believe?

Who will take from his hand jewels bound in a kerchief
that would save the beautiful soprano? He thinks

the watery curve of her whispers is a revelation.
Curious, how his life is mirrored in music. A light

from somewhere in the wings, upon the swells
of violins. The morning he feared would arrive.

That growing tide of chord upon chord .... Yes,
someone will be murdered—there's a dagger

in the folds of the diplomat's cloak. Done
since Act Two, while voices swirl like leaves

the courier clowns in his Stetson stage left, signaling
beers all round. The coachman places his bet.

Derek Mong

An Ordinary Evening in San Francisco

Goodnight children my kid met at the playground.
Your pajamas wait like starfish on your small beds back
   home.
Goodnight street sweeper, hugging

every odd-numbered hillside. Goodnight
tomcats, marching from the Marina to the moon.
We are leaving, we are leaving, we'll not be back soon.

Tonight the lit windows only lead
to better lives and other windows. They spread
out like the cell signals shooting through this night air.

Goodnight strobing cyclist, cyclops in the near-
darkness. Goodnight bald man counting out bus fare for
   his son.
We are leaving, we are leaving, we'll not be back soon.

And now the last dealers disappear
into their nondescript doorways; and their dead friend
drinks the cognac they left him on the curb.

We carry this evening to a back booth
at Tosca; we drink Irish coffee and sketch out bus routes,
long as tablecloths, to anywhere we'd call home.

The bartender sees himself in the table he's wiping
but still hasn't noticed that we've stolen his miniature
   spoon.
We are leaving, we are leaving, we'll not be back soon.

We leave and start walking. We say goodnight
to the smartphones swimming upstream like salmon.
Goodnight umbrellas, jostling for your six feet of dry air.

We crowd into a BART car that breathes underwater
and feel our eardrums dissolve. My son sees this crush
of bodies as a chance to try counting. We tell him

we are leaving, we are leaving, we'll not be back soon.

Jacob Minasian

Past Midnight
After van Gogh's The Night Café

An unfinished game
watched by light.
Electric eyes observing
shoulders lowered
by labor's vacuum,
eased by spirits, tumblers
glowing in sightline fires
capturing talk made
through movement.
Even the ones who stand
apart stand as part.
Time stands remote, too,
fast and slow, tired, hanging
above the conjunctive unknown,
known being out of sight,
beyond attention. A woman,
a man, an empty chair.
Everything watched by light
unwatched but seen.

III. Raise A Glass

Rick Smith

Real Poetry

I was still a kid.
It was late November on Route 413,
Pineville, Pennsylvania.
The ghosts were restless
on the porch of the general store,
the only store in town.
In the distance,
the sound of a hammer
ringing off cold steel,
pounding lonesome at dusk.
My Dad says, "son,
that's real poetry
right there."

Years after,
on the day we buried my Dad,
me and Bernie
raised a couple cold Rolling Rocks
at The Pineville Tavern,
the only bar in town.
We clicked those long necks
and talked about Dad.
He was with us for a moment.
There was motion, I swear
in that smoky tavern air.

Some guy down the bar
started mad-doggin' me.

Real poetry,
right there.

Amy MacLennan

It's Just a Tin of Squid

Wild caught,
in own ink
with some oil, salt,
a splash of tomato,
and I don't know what to do.
Some suggest pasta, garlic,
or maybe my father's sardine method,
on saltines with a cold beer.
But I'm afraid to flip the tab,
I suppose the way
I'm afraid to pull my own.
My father never drank
a cold beer, he drank six
along with Bloody Marys
more vodka than juice.
My ex said he never "promised"
to stay, and I hold onto that
instead of how he said
he wouldn't leave. I say
I'm fine with alone.
I say, I say, I say.
Things I tell myself,
packed in salt and ink.
I put the can on the shelf
then check the package
one last time, look
for an expiration date.
Find nothing.

Judith Barrington

The Thirstiness of Grief

1

Alone and thirsty for
    the blood of red wine
    the gold of brandy
    the fruits of sangría

one bottle after another until
they ushered in oblivion
and the tides carried me out
where the treacherous dead
filled their lungs and slept.

Thirsting for
    whiskey and gin
    tequila and beer
I sank down into weed and darkness
where nothing I wanted could be found.

I surfaced to sunlight and the morning cup
of foaming *café con leche*
but the new day's thirst grabbed
me once again by the throat.

2

I raced in my dead mother's car
down the burning road to Rosas,
burned in hot sun and fled into
the shade of my dead mother's umbrella.

I seared my shoulders crossing the bay
in a *pedalo* as I had done with her
years before in Caldetas.

Bars and café tables lined my routes,
champagne spilled over the laze of days.

    Tio Pepe said my dead mother
    Martini Blanco said the red letters on parasols
    Anis del Mono said my dead mother's
    best friend, Germaine

as if we were all really thirsty—
though we knew nothing of how
our parched throats would burn
with the array of poisons yet to come.

Jack Vian

The Forensic Sommelier

We acquire our habits like acquaintances
Of whose names we have quite forgot
Though we once knew them well enough
To smile when they laughed and to call
When they spoke of unbroken things, but
Somewhere along the cliché of now and when

They slipped through the likes of our typing bones
Leaving only frozen fragments on the nibless tips
Of our game yet sputtering tongues, like the seedless
Aftertaste of a ghostly wine, once as sadly sweet
As a lost and broken tune, but now bound far beyond
Our lips repair, except, perhaps, when caught betwixt
And unawares—like when the thought of your empty hand
Reaches out for an empty glass of empty air.

Karen Vande Bossche

Grief Like Alcohol

Your death, like
tequila, stings,
slides inch
by inch
to my stomach;
bringing water
to my eyes,
a gasp.

Tequila
will surprise me.
Yet I know
with salt, lime,
each successive
swallow numbs
the jolt,
deadens
the present.

Will salt
rubbed
in the wound
of you
dull the ache
of time
and tears.
Will I continue
to swig
with eyes
closed

until my lips
taste
the worm.

Rancid Blood

Jesus asked him, saying, "What is your name?" And he said,
"Legion," because many demons had entered him.
—Luke 8:30, New King James

You sit across the table and smile
Eyes dark, glazed, fingers tap the table
as I search for words
What is your name?

A worm crawls inside
eats the innards, of a rotten, soggy soul
You are dead, the you I knew
died years ago

If only I could cast out demons
and send them swine,
alcohol no longer your blood

So sorry, I have no words
The sight of you has stolen them
All I can do is hold your hand
I cannot climb your mountain
I cannot walk your path
I cannot fight your fight
This is a demon you must
cast out of Yourself
everyday

Michael Schein

Shot of Uriah

Ryely—
not O'Reilly
and not meanin clever,
but whiskey'd from toes to whiskers
is how Uriah died
and's how I'm writin this.
He'd think me a fool for cryin over him
but he'd join me in a drink to his burial
and whisper me his theory on funerals
how they're just weddins
for the devil and the dead.
He had a theory bout theories too,
that anyone with less than one
on everythin wasn't thinkin,
and a theory bout drinkin,
that it was yin to the yang of pissin,
then his theory on pissin
somehow linked it all back to thinkin
but beats me how.

"Amber ambrrrosia" he toasted,
the R rollin round the room,
pretzel dust dancin with his stubble,
"drives the dreamer sane,
and humbles philosophers,"
he philosophized, risin,
shakin his head at the shot in his hand.
"Rye makes live men dead,
and you can't get much humbler than dead"
he said, shakin the shot at his head,

swallowin,
smilin,
and proving it.

Michelle Cristiani

You, Me, Mommy
for Nikki Giovanni

Mommy said
God knew what he was doing when she was born white
because she was angry enough
for the world
already

When I was a little girl
in my "BJK is #1" tee shirt
Mommy would say:
Nikki, meet Mikki
Mikki, meet Nikki
and we would shake hands
your big book in my little fingers
and I learned, then,
that when you're angry, you don't shout:
you sing.

You sought beer while we poured whiskey
But we all of us were telling stories
with strong women ahead and behind
singing them to our people
and anyone who would listen

I want to thank you
I want to thank you again
But I know what you would say:
don't thank me
Thank your mother
Because God made her angry enough
to make the world better
for you

Marsha Mathews

Stuck
Wise, Virginia, U.S.A., 1996

Arriving at church, we found the side wall crumpled,
my daughter's Mitsubishi Eclipse smashed,
motor running,
Alanis Morrissette blaring.
Stained glass crunch-scraped beneath our shoes.

Found her
bloodied and dazed
humped over the steering wheel,
sixteen

Bud Lite cans, vomit,
green diet capsules scattered,
sirens humming.
From the rearview mirror,
pink and black ribbon,
an angel pin

ticked

wondering
who she'd blame
this time.

Mary Christine Kane

Drinking Mug

It could fit two beers
if I drank the foam quickly.
I laughed and argued and politicked
holding the mug like my talisman.

After the last gulp,
my reflection would surprise me:
just my tender eye.
Sometimes I would hold there a moment
letting myself rest in my sadness,
before pouring two more.
Gaining courage with every mouthful.
Edifying my audience.
Displaying my wit.
Never having enough.

Mark Donnelly

Imitation Drinking

I sit at the bar scribbling down poems
on cocktail napkins.
The romance of the writer
flowing from the whiskey
I rarely drink. Tonight I am
my father or one of my uncles.
Ray Milland in The Lost Weekend.
Give me another.

Missing my family, my life,
out of step with my present
and looking back at the past too much,
I pretend I'm a character in a novel or movie,
turn up my jacket collar and order another and another,
and one more before walking toward the Palisades,
searching for a future in the night.

Allen Braden

Both Portraits

In his bleary memory she poses
like an immaculate mannequin,
her eyes pimentos, joints frozen
in a gesture he's grown to know.

Loss is like a bluebottle fly
buzzing around in a mug of bourbon.
She'll come back. Any minute,
he keeps telling himself.

One day pours into the next
but he can still see her.
A dark square nailed to the wall.
A portrait taken down for good.

Jennifer Hambrick

Booze Run

and the octogenarian aunties arrive
and one settles into
a pink flowered nightie
and hair curlers
and the other's in a grey sweat suit
and they send me
to the liquor store—
vodka and tomato juice
for the one with the curlers
and cheap hooch whiskey
croaks the sweat suit auntie
and Mom says
get bourbon for mint juleps
we're from Kentucky remember?
and the air is cracker crisp
and tall paper bags
crunch with chill
and the aunties curl up
with their drinks
and the sweat suit auntie
swigs down
her vitamin pills

Jane Alynn

Grandmother

Her knotted hands
held the coppery needles
that flew like winged pencils
given a chance to settle the past
in the deepening act of repetition—
knit one, purl one,
each stitch a memento
of agony, catastrophe and shame
in our woolly genealogy
I knew little of until then.

I listened close—

picking up like dropped stitches
those bits of missing history
of hard life on the Iron Range,
our orchard's failed harvests,
grandfather's drunken rages
with no hangovers,
and her only child, my mother,
running away with a dancer
at fourteen, the second man who had her.

On the last row, she lifted
the river of yarn, rippling and restless,
its worsted weight falling away,
and, Circe-like, surrendered
her wands to show me the way
each stitch looped back
and that it didn't have to be endless.

Ed Werstein

German Style Lunch Break

Uncle Fritz is on his Ford tractor
mowing hay in a field near the house.
It's hot, and dry, and noon.
I'm about four. Mom is busy
with three younger kids.
Dad is at the Ford plant.

Mom puts a ham sandwich
a cold bottle of Pfeiffer Pilsner
and a bottle opener
in a brown paper sack
and gives me instructions.

Just walk out to the edge
of the field and wait for the tractor
to come 'round. When he sees you,
hold up the bag. I do as I'm told.

Fritz slows the tractor to an idling stop
dismounts and walks over to me.
Tells me to wait. He's sweating beads,
his shirt wet, his hat dripping.
He opens the bag,
eats half the sandwich,
opens the beer, drinks half,
eats the other half sandwich,
finishes the beer, puts the empty
and the opener back in the bag
and tells me to thank my mom.

He trots back and drops the Ford
into gear, engages the mower blades
lets out the clutch and takes off.

The whole thing takes less than three minutes.

Pick

The local boys I tagged around behind
those days what with the war
the great depression both fought
grubbing in the dirt between
belt tightening and shell shock

had enough farming to last them
said the old ways were done
even with the GI Bill to fall back on
no craving to get them a place
slap up a house go to college
if you were single why bother
the ground planting anything

so into their thirties and forties
most sat around drinking beer
playing poker talking girls and cars
studied each hand for the omens
allowed they were looking to get on
road crew construction what have you
or best of all the distillery
a river town forty miles off
where to hear the boys tell it
every man-jack worked a pick

which like as not would amount
to a little medicine bottle
with a string round its neck
that hung from the top buttonhole
of your bib overalls
down inside the stovepipe legs

so you could stand by the vat
stirring sweeping drop your pick
let it fill slowly pull up
lower down your pantsleg
wander off to where
you could duck down take a nip

and round their penny ante game
these layabouts heard tell
only lucky ones never got caught
and how day shift and night shift
most worked drunk
and what a joy that must be
to never feel a blessed thing
at the whistle stagger out
already a load on
not a soul sniping at you
your whole day or night still ahead

J.I. Kleinberg

Grandmother's Kitchen

She could brew a potion
that would round every vowel
in your teen-tough vocabulary,

that would sluice bruises
from jaw and knuckles
easy as berry juice.

With the first swallow,
which was neither cold nor warm,
sweet nor bitter, you begin

to forget the throb
of the afternoon's injury,
the meaning of words

exchanged in fury's glare,
the hot engine of fists
clenched deep in pockets

then urgent and pounding.
With another swallow,
your neck turns liquid,

your heels slide
from beneath your chair
along the suddenly slippery floor.

Your arms yield to a new gravity,
following your hands, loose
and heavy, downward,

your clamorous story—
vanquished, heroic—
a smear wiped from your mouth.

Braids

Puttering, pouring wine, rummaging
among the vacant objects
at midnight, the loose reminders
of all her marriages, markers—
before Henry, after Paul—
and now only the objects,
the salt shaker encrusted
with grease and grit,
the footstool she used to climb,
grabbing for cereal boxes
between stale crackers, baking soda,
cornstarch, tea.

Hadn't she worn swallows' wings,
chided the other birds,
refused to bend, to give in
and in? Hadn't she plaited her hair
with meadow grasses, dipping
her long-limbed body into morning lakes?

Her brandy glass has fallen
off her bed, the objects
of her sleep lie by her side.
It is no longer night.
It is no longer winter night.
Now she is no longer lying in her bed.
She has lost herself in herself.
She is reading her own mind.

Jathene

In the 1980s, my mother legally changed her name.
Jathene is a combination of her given name Jean
and the Greek goddess Athena.
She chose no last name. She couldn't find one to fit.

1.

Jathene is not
my mother's
birth name.

Her parents gave her
three names
and called her many others

It took me a long, long time
to call my humming bird
mother, Jathene.

2.

When she bought
her Santa Fe house, Jathene
was dressed in black wool.

She wore a Navajo fetish necklace
of coral and turquoise: carved bulls,
coyotes, seals and birds on a string of beads.

As she sat across from the agent,
ready to sign Jathene
on a deed of trust,

the woman behind the desk
pushed away her voice
clanging like dropping coins.

She said: *The form requires*
a first and last name.
This is a legal document.

Unruffled, mother sang
her hummingbird song
It is legal to be Jathene.

From there, she wore
gardenias, roamed Hawaii,
sipping Mai Tai, eating coconuts.

She ventured into Greece
and Crete, brought back
olives and wool

She breathed honeysuckle,
and gathered avocadoes and figs
in Santa Barbara, the mission town

where I grew up. There a banker said:
What's your name again?
I didn't catch the last name.

Before mother spoke
I interrupted to joke:
Her first name is Ja,

Her last name is Thene.
Ja   Thene!
He examined mother

as a fixed specimen
and not knowing in which
box to mount her wings

Squinting, he said:
What nationality
did you say that was?

3.

Today her ashes sit
in my writing room
in a copper urn beside

my favorite photo of her.
She smiles, white-haired
and young, wearing

a purple print dress
earrings dangling,
her matching coat

draped across a wicker
chair. Her hazel eyes
hold laughter.

I recall orange blossoms
and a humming bird's
flapping wings as it suckles.

I see the creek that borders
my childhood home and roams
from the mountain to the sea.

For me, an unnamed creek,
a moist soil for dry boulders
fallen oak leaves and children's feet.

In the photo, the restaurant's
bar and mirror reflect light
and I think:

Ja is part body
Thene is part myth.
My mother's name is Jathene.

C.J. Prince

Don't

Friday night's they forget
the *"don'ts."*

Don't is the first word
I remember—a voice from above.
Don't doesn't mean anything
if you're eighteen months old.

Adults on the couch laugh,
sip martinis. I reach
for the giant green olive
with a pimiento dot
like a comic book eye.
Mother's stern look flashes
a warning that might alert father.
I wait, play with wooden blocks.

Mom pulls out a cigarette, Dad flicks a Zippo.
A blue haze circles around me. They drink
and then an empty glass is lowered.
I snatch the shiny green treasure,
suck tart juice, bite into the chilled olive.
Martini juice dribbles to my elbow.

Susan Kelly-DeWitt

Headlong Down to Whiskey

My mother warned about the dangers of drink.
She said alcohol drenched my genes, my blood.
She predicted that even if I seemed to think
I could escape, I never would.

I was young and too rebellious to brood
much on her prophecies, meant to punish,
I thought then, though now I see her words
hid the fear I would inherit Father's death wish.

How to explain a life's weird pastiche?
My father drank himself to death before fifty.
I tossed the ritual clods into his grave-ditch.
Next a brother went headlong down to whiskey.

I've outlived them both by thirty-plus years.
Friend, let's celebrate that—I'll buy the beers.

John Krumberger

Beer

My father drank cheap beer his whole life.
Who knows where he found
his watered-down discount labels,
subject of countless jokes,
from his progeny as we grew older
and fancied ourselves knowledgeable
about choices in the world.

Now I have a daughter in her twenties,
who considers me out of step,
and maybe I am.
Every January she joins me
to visit his grave,
stopping first at a liquor store,
trying to be subtle
since you can't just ask
for the worst can of beer in the place.

This year we brought him an Old Style,
then drove through a snow squall
that lit up the sky on a country road
bound for Holy Family cemetery.
Neither of us wore boots,
striding the dark winter meadow
past gravestones, guided by the light
of her cell phone,
she placing the beer in front of him,
then stepping aside to allow me time
to tell him about the year.

Just then I looked up
to something flashing

in the fogged darkness;
both of us afraid to walk towards it,
though we did—in that little city
full of so many of my people—
discovering blue Christmas lights
hooked to a generator,
then draped over a grave
that drawing closer we found belonged
to my cousin, Mary Bodi.

I never knew her
except in childhood,
yet there she was and there I was
with my own child,
still puzzling out this world,
surprised at how happy I was
to receive the dead
with their jests and surprises.

Bryce Emley

College Beer

the wreck and not the story of the wreck
the thing itself and not the myth
—Adrienne Rich, "Diving into the Wreck"

New in a town where every bar is a dive,
I come to feel familiar somewhere dimly lit,
soaked in Willie Nelson's lilt,
floors cue-ball-scuffed, a basket
of condoms by the door.
I ask what they've got and stop her
when she gets to Schlitz.
Before I break the can open I conjure

my father sneaking
The Beer That Made Milwaukee Famous
into an Oral Roberts dorm, mid-June
Oklahoma storm, taking a girl out
to his first Austin-Healey,
dwelling in that space of time he lived
the stories he tells.

Bitter, tinny, it tastes like college beer.

Two decades after the hemorrhage,
only half his body heeding his will now
and nothing new to say,
every year for him is a stroke
toward the surface, swimming
out of the wreck, the thing itself
bluing into myth.

The Thing He Secreted

He spilled his childhood secret, imitating
a drunken TV clown, gulping Vodka—
bicycle ride & tumbled head to curb—amnesia.

He spoke of moonshine, sneaking
into Idaho bars; a father forsaking wine—
I want to make sure I can quit.

His bent: loitering outside groceries,
slipping bills to *old folks* for purchase
of illegal six-packs swilled in the park.

My love for you, he said, *can hang tight
until after the wedding.* We donned beer-cap
monocles and ran butt naked through

the campsite; Rosé in a bota bag, flasks
of Southern Comfort tucked inside our Kelty
packs. My family once adored his twinkling

eyes, now heads wag: Stingers, Colt 45s,
Strawberry Mead from the liquor store. Hardly
a secret, our quest for a shared life, me

ignoring his bent until too late; staggered
by grief, we raised crystal liqueur glasses,
toasting his life with syrupy Crème de Cacao.

Andrew Shattuck McBride

Jim Beam, Water, Ice

Jim Beam, water, ice. Dad's drink.
He kept the gallon bottle of whiskey
in the cupboard above my cereal
and box of powdered milk.

I don't remember Dad ever saying,
It's mine. Leave it alone.
Jim Beam whiskey, unmistakably his.
I never told him, *The cereal is mine.*
Leave it alone. The powdered milk, too.

The one expression of his I loathed:
You might want to know this someday.
I found it oppressive; I wanted only books.
I declined all instruction
he could have provided if I'd asked.

In my twenties, Jim Beam, coke, ice
became one of my drinks.
Dad was only sixty-seven when
he died in 1993. I've had to figure
things out on my own. Sometimes I can't.

Dad, what I wouldn't give for more
conversations, to ask you for advice,
to ask you how to do something.
I learned, late—in my early fifties—
that Jim Beam is sweet.
Jim Beam, water, ice. My drink.

Sarah Brown Weitzman

Bourbon

To amuse her and her little brothers
he'd whistle his pungent breath
into the narrow opening of his bottle
when it was almost empty, the sound
resounding like fog horns on the river
when all the boat traffic halted
and he had no work.

Other times before he'd had too many swigs
he would rub his finger around the rim
to make a piercing ring until they would screech.
But when the hunger was upon him,
worse than those hungers they understood,
he found no play in the bottle.

Then he'd explain how much he wanted to stop
and would.   Tomorrow.   This is the last,
he'd tell them, holding the bottle in the sunlight
so that it cast gold coins on the wall
until they could see so clearly
what was beautiful
and what was not.

Mary Eliza Crane

My Father's Sweater

I wear my father's sweater
colored by Irish sheep
though he has been dead more than three years.

I see him now
in the portrait of me as a poet.
Pointed chin,
Celtic nose,
his fine sand hair.
Our eyes turn inward now.

I am one year older
than when he downed his last drink.

He would not be happy
I am no longer married,
would rather write than work.
I still sit in the woods.

He remains my father
though I have lost the quality
of daughter.

It is my sweater now.

Marc Swan

Standing Tall

The night before the wedding
was quite an affair. My usually
conservative father drank drafts
with us at the Duchess, laughed
like hell when we stole the pool cue
at Uncle's Place, drank some more
at the Trade Winds, helped me up
when I fell off the bar stool
at the Tavern, kept the pace
when we went to the Gag & Heave
for fries and gravy and on the way back
to the motel, I could see him
in the rear-view mirror, sitting
between Hound and Carl, taking long
slow hits off a bottle of Dewars.
He was laughing at a lot of things
I'm sure he didn't understand.
The next morning I was dog tired.
He roused me at six am
for a prenuptial service and stood tall
beside me when I slipped on
that narrow gold band.

Jeff Walt

Kitchen Music

Friday nights my mother would slip in an 8-track
of Elvis, Patsy, Loretta, or Hank. We'd belt out
country hits and hymns, lip-sync Conway Twitty. I'd beg
to stay awake, cut in, scream the words,
a kid in flannel pajamas putting off sleep and dreams.
The men with us those nights—Vic and Henry
and Mac and Jim—would lift me with one hand above
old, torn linoleum, the smoke and laughter.
Mama danced the jig in bare feet and blue jeans,
hands in her hair—wild, like that feral cat we put down.
Her bra strapped to the back of her chair,
wearing her favorite T-shirt, "PA Girls Do it Best."
I swayed in their discordant toast,
cheered my mother's blue-black widow's peak.
We'd croon "Coal Miner's Daughter" and "Heartaches,"
each man louder and louder.
I puffed Winstons, sipped Schlitz, stole dollar bills
from their pockets. Ended up on my mother's lap,
riding her knee. We laughed at nothing, cussed
because we knew God was listening, sang until
we were asleep on the kitchen floor tangled
in the hum of each others' betraying arms.

Meg Kearney

Juncos

I can't pour this bird seed from cup
to feeder without seeing my mother
pour a Scotch. I
can't.

After they cut out her lung
I said, "I'll call you every day."
She said, "Did you call
then hang up?"
"Don't bother," my brother said,
"she never remembers."

Now I'm standing on the back deck
of the house in New Hampshire,
a cup of bird seed in my hands.

Now I'm standing on the roof
of my old building on East 20th Street
watching the Towers fall.

Now I'm sneaking into my childhood
home in LaGrange, thinking
of juncos. Their grey-white bodies
like a building smoldering.

Bird seed turns golden, poured into
morning air.

Bird seed is not whiskey, but—.

"Bird seed—it's in your hair,"
my mother said, reaching for me.

188

Matthew Sisson

Elephant in the Room

The elephant in the bedroom will always
keep you awake, be grateful it sleeps
on the floor.[1] The one in the kitchen ate
Triskets and ice cream, pizza and cake,
is still hungry, and searching for more.[2]
The elephant in the basement found
the vodka you drink there, promises
only to guard it.[3] The one in your
son's room is addicted to pills, copped
his stash, and was tempted to try it.[4]

---

[1] The poet was not a philanderer, but his constant raging ultimately
eliminated non-essential bedroom activities, and soon after, his
marriage.

[2] i.e. His ex-wife loved chocolate. Ate one or two small chocolate
covered pretzels for desert, leaving the rest of the bag for him.
Since moving out, he keeps no "bingables," and has lost (40) pounds.

[3] As his marriage fell apart, the speaker took up scotch, began
inviting people over as an excuse for further drinking. Drank his
daughter's kindergarten teacher under the table. Confronted by his
then wife, he went through a month or two of denial, but before
thorough addiction, gave it up completely.

[4] Thankfully, none of the speaker's children has ever had a drug
problem. Still, substance abuse is close to his heart.

Classic Cocktail

Moonlighting as bartender, my father
Bungled home with lipstick on his collar,
Having steadied one tipsy regular
On stiletto heels to her Impala.

No surprise he deflected Mother's glare.
It wasn't the first time he'd come home kissed.
He balled the telltale Van Heusen, then missed
The jump shot into the wicker hamper.

Dad taught me how to mix a martini:
Swirl vermouth in the shaker, snap it fast.
Over cracked ice, pour four fingers of gin.
Stir then strain into the chilled cocktail glass.

Add one pimentoed and toothpicked olive.
Sip until the divorce papers are served.

Jeanne Yeasting

Cheat or Not

Hearts were cheap
or so our parents must have
thought the night they bought
that damn slick-sided,
twenty-five-foot fiberglass

pleasure craft, giving
us a twenty to go
amuse ourselves.

Gin was what
we bought—no one thought
to card us. Tonic,
enough

to set our spirits up
a notch, even though
the oldest of us was bound
to beat any of us

playing hearts, cheat or not,
trying to make points.

Who'd have thought
that boat would sink?

First days, the hull cracked.

Katherine Gekker

Alcohol Beckons Constantly, Derails

each and every day earlier and earlier. Your breakfast
  juice—
firewater, which means forlorn me, followed by
medicinal
gimlet. You're ginned up long before cocktail
hour, hosed by metallic vodka,
ice cubes clinking against cut crystal, those
jazz jezebels jockey with your reason. Your mind, the
  whole
kit and caboodle, goes kablooey. You say,
let the drinking begin. I say, *you lush, it never stops, look in the*
mirror—that's you smashed by margaritas.
Not that you drink indiscriminately. No, you nurse
only one rule—keep drinking. You
pour another, pursue your pickled
quest, a quagmire of doctored quinine.
Righteous, rigid, ruined in rum, you turn to
Scotch, sloshed, snookered. Can I remain stoic?
Trashed, you tumble under the table,
useless. You're
vacant, veer away from me, seek vermouth—
weeping, whiskey-wasted, wankered. I long to be an
ex,
yearn to unyoke from you, you
zonked zombie. Soon, I will swing from
                    a crystal
                chandelier,
            catapult
        through the
    open
window and disappear into the night: Zorro.

Carrie Albert

Ant Motel

A man seated next to me on the bus opens
his book to share photos of a pharaoh's tomb.

Bright red wounds on his hands are as perfectly
round as dimes. He kindles conversation.

We are both California natives, miss
hikes in rolling hills where spring

green turns to summer hay perfumed
with sage. He asks, *If I clean up,*

stay with the program, will you go
with me to see the ants? He's not o.k.

but I act as if. Perhaps an ant farm resides
within his mind that strives

for industry and order not unlike mastery
of slaves who built the pyramids.

Maybe naive, I tell him about
a garden made by children where I saw

Ant Motel handwritten on a miniature
stone archway amid crumblings of cheese.

Inside puffy lids, blue irises
are washed paler than I've ever seen.

He sips from a canteen scented of my past.
I ask, *Is something troubling?*

He opens his private tomb: *ruptured disc—pills*
don't stop the pain—my mother died last year—

your hands are so small. I'm drawn back to
the round/stabbing push/pull of intoxicated touch.

I once hoped a *program* or love itself
would be enough. He smiles farewell

then steps out into a storm.
Dear orphan, who will mother you?

Liz Bruno

Drink

There are so many ways to ruin something good.
　So few to make it right.

I stopped believing in wine a long time ago:
The corkscrew too easy, the swallow too smooth
on any Friday night in some dim-lit kitchen,
tired restaurant, deserted dormitory.

That medicine is all the same. Rx: Drink me
As if anywhere with anyone could mean
anything. And after awhile you start to learn,
like the rooster, how hard it is to rise again.

I cannot drink that drink, face that fatal flow
of things kept compartmentalized. One bottle
a meal, one man a bottle, one nothing in the end
and so American it goes; alone, alone, alone.

There is a kind of love that kills, and, yes,
there are other things. The sweaty palm
of the local boy as he extends the portafilter,
under pressure to finish what others have begun.

Twenty hands around the cup he passes off.
Melting pot: four countries and forty traditions
swimming together in a 27-second stream,
Medicine stronger than being self-made.

I used to sip down one man's vineyard until
I realized: One man will always let you down.
I've begun to believe in somebody else's fingers
in lost privacy, and in the daily certainty of error.

In the end, someone will always let you down.
On that day, a normal day, I hope you find yourself
brushing hands with the eager twenty-something
smiling softly as he sees the crema start to slide.

Carol Alexander

First Drunk

Drunk is a field ridged with white stones that hummock
   up crude,
and you are sixteen, stumbling into the divots incised
   by hooves.

Drunk is the leather coat of a boy, lax where it's hung
   on a peg for years,
the coat of the father who needs it no more.

Thirst that grows where it should be slaked, snow
   muffling the tongue:
only to bloom again in the bottle, the coiled worm so
   cold.

First drunk, the stars split and crumble, carve out a
   sickle face.
This spectral ground, void of life—where are the crows,
   the silky mice?

They're webbed in branches, or under the earth, and
   the leached sky
quivers to the thrum and his mouth, like a horse's, is
   apple to taste.

And his mouth like a horse's is soft to the bit, and long
   bones
shudder for the crop, the tequila's blue burn, the
   muddy embrace.

And night is a barn fragrant with oils, the heat of the
   mares;

it's a lonely moon that peers through his eyes and
filches a draught of sun.

Kateri Kosek

Manhattan

This is life, isn't it, this standing around in kitchens
        taking stock
            of last night's damages
which won't dissolve like the sweet cocoa
    I whisk into simmering milk
                the hot chocolate we make to put off
what really needs to be done, cinnamon
    and vanilla
            floating between our words

this stumbling into morning, quiet 5 a.m. streets
        the frozen fields
                beside the church whose services
I'll sleep through, bells and all
            rocking in a rough
                    whiskey sleep
no dreams of you for whom I never
        longed
                despite the snapping fire and
        the people thronging on the cold dark streets
I wandered alone
            looking
        for something I didn't want to find
            not really
    and the gypsy bright
cave of the restaurant, the cocktails
            you insisted on, the first ones

            then our faces disappearing
        as the logs burned down

the caramel-colored drinks depleted,
        the room dark like you like it
the cherry glistening at the bottom of the
    Manhattan.

IV. One for The Road

Laura Sweeney

Starry Night
For Davre

In the starry night of January—Oregon
I sip pinot in my friend's hot tub
inhale the evergreens and
sketch memories of visits long ago.

As I sip pinot in my friend's hot tub
I recall a summer's day when
we sketched memories
of our youth and whimsy.

Like a summer's day
free from vulgarity
I was whimsical and carefree
from Iowa's winter brambles.

But vulgarity chilled
as swirling colors changed in hue
like Iowa's winter brambles
to garish blue and yellow.

Swirling colors changed in hue
to shadows
of garish blue and yellow—
a post-accident life.

Shadows and
years
of post-accident life.

Now, our banter is not the same.

But he holds my moonlit body
as I inhale the evergreens
soothed
in the starry night of January—Oregon.

Jeffrey Alfier

Winter Stopover
Childersburg, Alabama

Night should smell like bedstand flowers.
Like Norfolk Southern's groaning freight.

But it's dankness, barroom Formica,
a town forever flying a half-mast flag.

Some barstool angel holds a hard
eye on me from across the room.

She detects I'm a weak and easy catch,
and so we're off to her flat.

We pass through her kitchen. A moonbeam
warms the wall clock.

Our passion is spent in spades. I toss
with the edgy slumber of restless travelers.

Come morning, sky ladled by storms, I look
through the bedroom window to her backyard.

A toy left outside fills with rain.

Carol Steinhagen

The Road Taken

Their red car holds the broken road,
cutting sharp curves that threaten
to propel it into the darkness of hemlock.

A pothole drops it down, hard.

He curses, presses the gas pedal.

She stares at the seedlings growing stubbornly
out of roadside boulders, at starry chicory,
at little clouds of plastic bags
fluttering down from trees to guardrails.

We need more beer, he says, shifting gears.
She adds beer to the list folded in her purse
and remembers duct tape
to cover the crack that let in the bat.

Around the next bend lies the relief
of green meadow edged with rabbit foot's clover.
She wants the strange banded cows to be there—
the Belted Galloways that make the field a landscape
with their pure strokes of black and white.

Kenneth Bennight

Pasture at Dusk

On the horizon
the setting sun tints
stratus clouds rosy orange

In front of the stratus clouds,
gray cumulus ride a high wind
to the north

Closer than the streaming cumulus,
trees in a thick stand languidly sway
with a lower, softer waft

In front of the trees,
the insect orchestra tunes its instruments
as the open pasture slides into dusk

I, puffing a mellow cigar,
sip a stout
and behold the display

Ekphrasis
inspired by Flegel's A Dessert Still Life

1.

In a still life with grapes and other points of interest,
the eye goes to a glass chalice on a tabletop,
notices how those grapes glisten, though not more so
than the chalice, sparked by ceremonies of light;
how just a few arcs of white, scrapings really,
stoke our curiosity.
You almost have to dip a finger in to find out
if it's empty or not, so fragile is the distinction
between glass and wine.
Ask yourself if we aren't like that, holding emptiness
in an invisible embrace, downing it
in a thirst for light.

2.

But this is only part of the picture.
That stilted parrot, for instance, why is it robed
in the varnished dark?
The white dot on the eye of the mouse
offers a glimmer of an answer.

3.

Is it greed that gives the gray mouse its appetite
for sticky fruits and nutmeats?
Or is it desire, the dark in the light that enthralls us
and gives us weight?

Ann Tweedy

when she looks into my eyes

i am grapes whose tendrils
wind around trellises in a prized
vineyard. the owner walks
the grounds satisfied—
the weather has been
kind this season. many years
from now, wine from these unplucked
berries will be impeccable. the grapes
clustered on the vines somehow feel
this. they know they are worthy,
that the sun, who nourishes
or deprives, has shined. what can
the grapes be but pleased
with themselves? does it matter
they simply drank in
what they were given?

Petrels

*Petrels don't walk on water...but they push themselves
along with their feet, looking as if they are walking on
the waves.*
—from *100 Birds and How They Got Their Names*

Our ship in its bottle is forever
tossed at sea. Two petrels follow
lee side. Two in our wake. There's
ice in the rigging; life-boats all are
fake. Petrels seem to walk on water
but skim the surface for our chum.
Each night we spew that over-
board, rinse our stinking mouths
with rum. I knew it was a dumb idea
to climb aboard this ship. Said it just
before you offered that first nip.
Before the petrels. Before the squall.
Before the bottle made us small.

David Radavich

Wine in The Ruins

Amid toppled Civil War tombstones
we settle our blanket
on a hill overlooking hills
at sunset
just after the rain.

The sausage is unpacked,
cheese, wine, the twice-missing forks,
and a certain anxiety about
the future.

Who used to walk here?

How did they live?

Why are they fallen now?

We don't talk about it,
or the weather.

We manage to comment
on everything but ourselves.

The shining whiteness of gravestones
smirks brilliantly aslant.

Shadows prod the dusk,
we gather blanket, and depart.

Who would have thought
this was the last time, the burial,
the affirmation of a division
seeking itself?

String of Pearls

Dave wears a string of pearls
as we watch his life
of Reality TV
over our dashboards
getting onto I-5.

Our guilt drips affluence
is jolted by confluence:
his eyes
rear ending our lives.

Money for beer
implores his sign
as Dave wonders
about honesty.

If we didn't look away
we'd see his pearls
simmer and glow
with images:
the Mekong Delta
and helicopters.

But they go dark
like a bottomless Vietcong pit.

The endless red light
suddenly turns green

and we race away

relieved to just have to face
our angry, illogical boss

...and Dave to never pray.

Diane Stone

Summer Solstice, Double Bluff

It's a wonder we care anymore,
knowing what we know about reversals,
changes of heart, second chances
hanging by a thread.
Watch out, kids, here comes fate
barreling down the drive,
brake fluid low, a distracted god
snoozing at the wheel.

There's more bad news:
some wrens have changed their tunes,
and whales are starving.
in a sea of plastic garbage.
Golden paintbrush waves goodbye
from the deck of a waning palette.
We might be next from what I read.

So we gather at the beach
with glasses of champagne
to toast this longest light
even if dark nods just around the bend.
The longest day's no sooner here
than it bails out too,
leaving us stranded
with our towels and doubts,
gulls shrieking overhead.

As we lay on our backs
beneath a carousel sky,
frowns soften, hands unclench.

What a spectacle we are—
slowly spinning on this crazy wheel
called now and forever and all at once.

Alice B. Fogel

Scotch

Tannins and embers of peat
hint at their contact
with a small cask's oak, smoke
in the hollow of a broad bay.
Doubly aged, chill filtered,
velvet edges at the surface
linger long in the finish.
From the valley of green grass
and malts of the highlands,
from the vale of meadows,
sweetness flavors the sap
with the tastes of mint,
freshly cut meadow flowers,
lemon, honey, comfort, closure.
A bit of salt, seaweed.
On the island shore,
in the rocky lee, barley distilled
with rind and myrtle blossoms
into an amber liquid flowing full
of golden poison for the soul.

Richard Widerkehr

At Playa Catalonia

Chefs with white hats tall as China Line ships....
Heaven's like that on the *playa*, girls in bikinis,
as my mother says, *One string above,*

One below. Why do they bother? Here
everyone's GPS is turned off. No maps,
just paths that go nowhere. It's possible to fall

in love over and over, without the pain
of being young. Linda isn't jealous.
After lunch, we bask as frigate birds

glide high like spiritual advisors
so deep in their mystique they won't tell us
which restaurant to eat in. In Tulum,

Mayans sacrificed in the Temple
of the Wind. Now we take a left,
a right. Music sifts through palm fronds,

fanning themselves. Small posts
throw dim light on our path. Coatis,
rodents with tails and an attitude,

beg outside the buffet, grub for bugs,
climb into the jungle. Heaven's
like that—how did we come here?

I sip my margarita. Two palm trees
bump and grind under moonlit clouds—
unearthly, yes. At dawn, waves of aqua

and lime-green say, *Forget, forget.*
Dark blue, farther out—maybe
we came from it, maybe not.

Jeffrey Alfier

Exiting a Bar in Crown Heights, Brooklyn

It may have been a winter night I chewed a final piece
of ice in a glass of Rittenhouse rye. Enough false
courage to follow freezing rain down an alley

without cats, without moonlight. There was no topo
map with its red, steep lines. No character
I'd name shady. No evidence of a broken life
or bottle. No secreted lovers polishing their sex.

Not even a siren crisscrossed that dark.
All was quiet, as if the alley had been granted
a façade of grace. Only a waitress on smoke break

under a faltering light above a deli's back door,
the beam flickering like an uncertain trumpet. I passed
her by. From wooden steps below the door, she exhaled
smoke, like a kiss blown from the railing of a ship.

Sheila Bender

At Snowfall

The weather brushes over our lives
as if they could be refinished,
snowflakes brightening in the moonlight
like details toward a punch line.

I remember one about a drunk
searching on the corner for keys
he'd lost a block away saying he
needed the light.

Love, like this snow, reflects back
all the light, our bald forsythia's branches
casting shadows like a net as if they shared
one skin with snow.

Come back to me. Come hold me again.

Paul Fisher

Honey-Drunk

While others make merry, we make mead.
—anonymous

When November wraps
her bones in leafless gowns,
and December stumbles
from the Twelfth Moon Saloon,
clover cowers, night malingers,
and thunder tunes its kettledrums.

That's when, honey-drunk
and banished to huddle in the hive,
bees bumble through a bar or two
of hummingbird song.

Anita K. Boyle

Ode to the Beer-Colored Moon

1. The Eclipsed Red
Our moon is a hermit crab,
ruthless and bitter.
He is in pursuit of a lavish vessel,
which he will pirate
as his new hidey-hole.

At last, this florid moon backs
into a plain brown bottle—
a burbling lunatic who looks
to protect his underbelly,
while his burgundy glove
grasps at anything dark.

2. Imperial Moon
This windy evening our moon
becomes a torpedo that soars
through black sticks for hour
after bellowing hour. Just
before dawn, she cozies up
to the sun, filthy
and bitter still.

3. Waning Crescent
Yellow, the moon
is the flavor of dandelion,
biting the throat,
bruising both tongue
and tonsils, a breath
not quite good enough.

4. Sunday's Summer Ale
The golden halo
of a honey-colored moon,
smells holier-than-thou, which
isn't so great. A few shabby holes
in the clothes tell the tale.
Plus, the leavings of mice.

5. The Bees Wax Gibbous
The new and ready-to-use
moon has training wheels
that buzz like bees. Flashy,
plastic strips trail behind
blowing in the breeze.

6. Last Quarter
Blind, yet quick as a kick,
a foul round shadow
moves across the yard,
and there is a sound—
a back-of-the-mouth
giggle—a cousin lost in the dark.

7. Hefty Moon
We quench our thirst with
the acrid moon. Savor
the strong, rosy floral,
its hint of honey. How about that
scotchless peat, with its finished
silken texture, the congruence
of burnt sugar? We write poems
about the moon because of all that.

8. Full Moon
"Love the glow, old boy,"
you shout to the sky. Golden,
the lucky moon burns
behind a thin curtain of clouds.
You praise its sheen, so startling,
like the scent of grapefruit
hanging tight to the charcoal trees
in the night. Surprisingly tart!

9. The Waning Porter
A darkling moon
sips ivory foam slowly all night,
bark-sweet and creosote-warm,
a dull glow fades away
like a wounded hound.

The last sliver of moon
in the morning
tastes of molasses
and blueberries.
Hunger follows,
voracious and fierce.

DeWitt Clinton

With the Sun Peeking onto the Lake
I Open the Shades and Read Su Tung P'o's
"Moon, Flowers, Man"

We don't get many visitors who
Stop by for a refreshing cold glass yet
Every drinking night I check what
Phase the moon is in, and where
It floats in the sky
Then give a quiet thanks for joy
But more for blooming lilacs,
All breathing beasts, all legged
Creatures who speak or don't utter
A word in French or Urdu or
Any speech we might
Use to toast the night
And forget all those who
Might break in to slit our throats.
Perhaps they'd like to try a new Pinot.

Jeremy Cantor

Lengthwise

Pinot needs constant care and attention. You know?
And in fact it can only grow in these really specific, little,
tucked away corners of the world.
—Paul Giamatti as Miles Raymond in *Sideways* (2004)
  Alexander Payne, director

We did the Valley lengthwise, north to south.
Calistoga down to Napa, easy
if you take it easy on the wine.

"Did you see the one
who poured the first flight of dry reds?
Those eyes could melt a man at twenty paces!
But I couldn't ask her out.
She's at work—
awkward for her, you know?"

"You could have given her your card," I told him.

"Why bother?
I'm not even in her league."

Another mile in silence
then a winery with roses at the end
of every row of comfortably old vines,
grapes hanging, waiting for the picking
and the crush.

The gates had closed at five
so it was easy to admire the wrought-iron tracery
against the background of the cellars, vines
and roses.

"Nice gates," he said.

I pointed out, "They're closed."

"That's how I know they're nice," he said,
cradling the bottle he'd just bought,
wishing he had sprung for the reserve.

Gretchen Fletcher

Just a Taste of Friendship

Down rows of espaliered vines now
in this season cut back
almost to stumps
past oak barrels stamped "Beaune"
to wood planks set on sawhorses—
makeshift tables for momentary friends
who like as not will never meet again.
We sit like lifelong pals and watch circles
of California sun float in our glasses.
Our laughter grows like our friendship.
The Cabernets are fun,
but then the Pinot Noirs become really funny
and make way for knee-slapping Chardonnays
followed by hysterical Zinfandels.
Our new-found friends become wittier
'til, the sun low, we vow to stay in touch
then go back down those rows
of vines and leave, forgetting
to exchange e-mail addresses.

Carol Gordon

A Week After Our Daughter's Wedding We Call a Plumber

One thing you can depend on
after a major family event
is bursting pipes. As if
we could maintain these manners
just so long.

Our last quarrel, we've decided
is a draw.

But we console ourselves,
according to the latest polls,
the president's in trouble, too.
His wife appears before the press in pink
with pearl buttons. Innocence
does not beguile us.

Weddings do.
We borrow for them,
diet, trim, and tuck it in.
We fall for it, gladly, once again.

On your knees under the sink
you curse the hardware,
the way they do things nowadays.
Who to turn to for advice?
We patch it up. We still have
a leftover bottle of champagne on ice.

Brian Cooney

No Fruit So Wonderful as Want

Her daughter wrote from camp about the dance.
A boy came up to let her know the guys
all thought she was the ugliest girl there.
Our waiter repeats the specials.
The Beaujolais arrives.
She'll have the sea bass with tomato and caper sauce.
The humidity rises in advance of midsummer storms.
How tiresome it is, she says, this heat.

The talk drifts to chickens. A neighbor keeps
a few in his backyard, where they brood
near a shared stone wall, live off table scraps.
Her husband sighs.
Coyotes can be a nuisance.
Awakened by squawks, the neighbor had found a hen
wedged half through a knothole in the coop floor,
strewn bones and viscera
in the fetid space below.

It is sickening, she blurts,
to watch that child eat.

Tod Marshall

Coyotes

Two coyotes near your house, the end of a long night of
    drinking,
one of those evenings that begin with crafted beer and
    end with three guys
at a dive sloshing whatever's on tap—Rainier, PBR, or
    Kokanee—
and debating whether anyone's tough enough to start
    ordering shots.
They are sleek creatures, jittery at a car door closing.
    Smart,
they often know when to avoid poison. Tonight, they
    are bold,
sniffing and trotting near as the red tail lights of your
    friend's car
round the corner and swerve a bit, overcorrecting to
    keep from hitting the curb.
Trickster, you say, as they edge closer, ears alert but
    hackles flat
and eyes decidedly nice, like a poodle-dog or a baby seal.
You put out your palm, flip it to let one sniff the back of
    your hand,
forgetting about the other one that earlier flashed a
    snarl.
The coyote sniffs, sniffs, then licks your knuckle,
and you lift your hand to stroke its back just as the
    other one rips
your Achilles. From the ground, the row of mailboxes
looks like a line of stiff letter Ps or lockjaw Fs
that say here, now, right here is a Feast. Hungover in
    the morning,
fizzy water and orange juice help. God, the day ahead is
    busy

and boring with routine. You wonder why your muscles
feel so tight—even your brain—you wish that some
    instinct
would take over your body, and later, sitting at a desk
    for work,
you feel an urge to twitch pulse through your legs, an
    urge to kick something
that becomes just pain, everywhere pain, but especially
    your lower calf.

Brian C. Felder

Evening Solace

Those days that end with an olive'd martini
enjoyed beside the fireplace are my favorites,
though any day that one ends alive is a good one.
Our own experience, mine hard won in Vietnam,
teaches us to never take survival for granted,
but even if you're still new to this planet
                                    or just naive,
all you need do is watch the nightly news
to know how tenuous all of this is.
The proverbial horsemen of the apocalypse
                                    never dismount,
never pause for food or drink or sleep, trampling all
beneath their muddied, bloodied hooves.
It is well when they pass you by,
either not seeing you where you stand
or thinking you unworthy of their time,
but they will be back this way another day.
And so I stay by my hearth, drink in hand,
and enjoy the moment, for it is but that.

Laura Sweeney

From the Gateway Hotel Patio

I note the slanted slate rock
underneath a Quaking Aspen grove.
I walk over with pen in hand,
sit down, exhale,
inhale the spruce and petunias,
the yellow zinnias and orange mums,
the lavender Russian sage,
feel the whoosh caress my nape.
A tiny red spider and a large black ant
tickle up my shin. I want to take it in,
because the summer heat
will soon devour the July grass.
I want to linger and listen
to the cicadas, crickets, crows
sing like the waterfalls in Norway
over sparkling stones, splashing on the ear
a chorus of relief that soothes
like a rain stick or a peach martini.
An asylum from my melancholy.
Let it take me.

Douglas M. Smith

Winter Light

On my way to dinner
I took the shortcut down
the brick passageway
behind the storefronts
of downtown, expecting
to go blindly through
the darkness

but a wedge of light
fell from the bookstore
window, bright enough
to warm the sidewalk

inside friends sat listening
to an expert offer advice
on how to write a bestseller

I stood in the alley
alone, looking in
at their determined faces
so earnest I wanted to cry

knowing I could have
joined them
but chose instead
a sautéed white fish
and perfectly chilled glass
of Sauvignon blanc

this was no rejection
of belles lettres
of friendship
I was hungry
for something else
that night
and willing to suffer
loneliness
for the pleasure

Sibyl James

Twisp, Washington

Back east, they'd call these foothills mountain,
but you learn to map a different scale here
where the road west of you keeps rising
into a pass closed Thanksgiving to April,
where yards of rusted Ford bodies
and wringer washers aren't lack of pride
but history to people that don't read books,
a comfort of real things to talk
and tinker about, drawing off the restlessness
that comes between Saturday nights.

You could live a good winter here,
rent rooms in any grey weathered house
and watch the snow shift on porch chairs
left out ready for spring. Eat venison
and brown gravy at the Branding Iron
every Sunday, and walk it off
on the ridge behind the old copper mine
with that pack of scavenger horses and mules
snorting at your heels, and your own breath clouds
frozen at your lips like cartoon speech.
You won't need much talk here
where the names of things get crystal
and definite as that frozen air, something to exchange
hand to mittened hand on the morning bridge.
"Neighbor" is the guy who takes your shift
the day the baby's born. "Love"'s the years
of Saturday nights she's held your head above the john.

When the sawmill shuts down, the quiet
goes sharp and ebony behind a fine mesh of stars.
The creek runs louder than the road then, a sound
drawing you out to walk until the frost patterns your
    eyes,
and the cold burns in your blood like a hunger
for coffee and wood smoke, turning you back to town.

In one good winter, you could get so solitary here
that you'd forget the name for lonely,
until the spring came, surprised you
like the sound of ice breaking under the bridge.
It would be the day you swept the snow from porch
    chairs,
the night you stayed past closing in the Branding Iron
while the waitress shared Wild Turkey on the house,
let you talk until she turned the empty bottle over,
smiling, handing you the news the pass was open,
like a word she'd dusted off that morning
and knew you'd just turned foreign enough to use.

Kake Huck

Pinecones, Venice

but there was nothing to write about / except
life and death / and the warning sound of the
train whistle.
—Billy Collins

Searching for concrete imagery,
I look out my window onto pinecones,
instead of marble, where asphalt

not water winds off to those stores and
restaurants I would enjoy much more
if only I were as rich as that poet laureate

full of wit and wine who writes of
cigarettes and sorrow but performs
like he's on Broadway while I'm stuck

staring at my front yard where pinecones with
their seeds and stickers, cement
like similes to my page and pen,

making a simple linkage I assume
you'll find profound after the punchline,
(I mean *the close*) when the mysteries

of home and travel (or do I mean life and death?
[and by life and death do I mean poetry?])
and our ambivalence to all that is

Italian
seems captured by the piney pitch
and Fibonacci spirals of the pinecones.

John Davis

Replenished

Red wine, not cranberries or liver,
replenished our blood. In the landscape
of late summer when moths had all gone tan

with dried grass, we poured and replenished
ourselves with wine that stained our teeth
and tongues, got us drunk before we fried

our chicken in lard or formed syllables
of love. We drank the red expressions
of women and men who clacked

their heels along the sidewalks. We drank
to dead friends: their memories sweetened
with raisins and honey. In time we drank

and did not get drunk but entered a house
of worship when we sipped exhaustion—
our holiness of the heart. Under the unpaid

bills and the wall clock that echoed
across kitchen tiles we drank wine
and made room for our lives.

About the Editor: James Bertolino

James Bertolino taught literature and creative writing for 36 years, and retired from a position as Writer-in-Residence at Willamette University in 2006. Bertolino's poetry has been appearing internationally in books, magazines and anthologies for well over 50 years. His first book was published in 1968, and his most recent of 27 titles appeared in 2014—which was *Ravenous Bliss: New and Selected Love Poems* from MoonPath Press.

Bertolino's poetry has been recognized nationally by the Book-of-the-Month Club Poetry Fellowship, the Discovery Award, a Hart Crane publication award, a National Endowment for the Arts fellowship, two Quarterly Review of Literature book publication awards and the Jeanne Lohmann Poetry Prize for Washington State Poets.

Twelve volumes and fifteen chapbooks of his poetry and prose have been published by such publishers as Copper Canyon Press, Carnegie Mellon University Press, New Rivers Press, Ithaca House (associated with

Cornell University), Bonewhistle Press (associated with
Brown University), Quarterly Review of Literature
Award Series (Princeton University), Cherry Grove
Collections, and World Enough Writers. Two of his out-
of-print books have been reprinted by the Connecticut
College Contemporary American Poetry Archive.

Bertolino holds an MFA from Cornell University, and
taught creative writing for over 36 years at Cornell,
Washington State University, University of Cincinnati
and Western Washington University, as well as at
Skagit Valley College, Edmonds Community College and
Shoreline Community College in Washington State. He
retired in 2006, following a year as Writer-in-Residence
and Hallie Ford Chair of Creative Writing at Willamette
University in Oregon.

Over a hundred magazines, including *Ploughshares,
Poetry, Notre Dame Review, Indiana Review, Partisan Review,
Florida Quarterly, Paris Review, Beloit Poetry Journal, Raven
Chronicles, StringTown* and *Crab Creek Review* have printed
his poems.

In addition, his work has been reprinted in 42
anthologies, including, *Poets Against the War* (The Nation
Books), *A Gathering of Poets* (Kent State University
Press), *New Poets of the American West* (Many Voices
Press), and *New Hungers for Old: One Hundred Years of
Italian-American Poetry* (Star Cloud Press).

Bertolino's most recent prose book is *The Path of Water,*
an interview-memoir conducted by Mathew Campbell
Roberts, 2008, Stone Marrow Press. He spent the
month of March, 2008, as a resident artist at the Espy

Foundation in Oysterville, Washington, where he also enjoyed a productive residency at Willapa Bay AiR in September, 2013.

He lives with his wife Anita K. Boyle—herself a poet, poetry publisher, and graphic designer—as well as a dog, a cat, and some chirpy birds on five rural acres near Bellingham, Washington.

Contributor Biographies

Carrie Albert is a multifaceted artist and poet. Her works have been published or upcoming in many diverse journals, some with curious names including: *cahoodaloodaling*, *FishFood*, *Weird Sisters*, *Sheila-Na-Gig* and *Penhead* (where she is a permanent fixture as Poet-Artist in Residence). She lives in Seattle with her poodles, rabbits, pigs, deer, and an elephant (her farm of papier-mâché projects).

Carol Alexander's work appears in anthologies including *Broken Circles* (Cave Moon Press), *Through a Distant Lens* (Write Wing Publishing), and *Proud to Be: Writing by American Warriors, Vol. 1* (Missouri Humanities Council and Warriors Arts Alliance). Her work can be found in various print and online journals. She is the author of the chapbook *Bridal Veil Falls* (Flutter Press). Alexander's full-length collection of poems, *Habitat Lost*, is due out in 2017 from Cave Moon Press.

Jeffrey Alfier's latest works are *Anthem for Pacific Avenue: California Poems*, *Bleak Music*—a photograph and poetry collaboration with Larry D. Thomas, and *Southbound Express to Bay Head: New Jersey Poems*. He is founder and co-editor of Blue Horse Press and *San Pedro River Review*.

Blaise Allen, Ph.D. is Director of Community Outreach, The Palm Beach Poetry Festival. Her poems have been widely published in literary anthologies and magazines including: *South Florida Poetry Journal, Clackamas Literary Review, Pulse Medical Review, East End Elements, Naugatuck River Review, The Meridian Anthology of Contemporary Poetry, Blue Fifth Review, Long Island Quarterly*, and *Mothering Magazine*.

"The Rapture" was first published by the *South Florida Poetry Journal*, Issue 5, May, 2017.

Luther Allen writes poems and designs buildings from Sumas Mountain, Washington. Writing poetry has become his form of spiritual practice. He facilitates SpeakEasy, a community poetry reading series in Bellingham and is co-editor of *Noisy Water*, a poetry anthology featuring 101 local poets. His collection of poems, *The View from Lummi Island*, can be found at othermindpress.wordpress.com. His next project is versifying a previously written non-fiction work about hunting.

David Alpaugh sips wine and watches birds in the San Francisco Bay Area, where he also teaches literature for the Osher Lifelong Learning Institute and writing for the University of California Berkeley Extension. His poetry, essays, and plays have appeared in more than 100 journals and anthologies and he has been a finalist for Poet Laureate of California.

Jane Alynn is a poet and photographic artist. She is the author of two collections of poems: *Necessity of Flight* (Cherry Grove, 2011) and a chapbook, *Threads & Dust* (Finishing Line Press, 2005). Her most recent award was Second Place in Georgia State University's Journal of Art and Literature, *New South*, poetry contest, in 2012. Her poems have appeared in numerous journals and anthologies, and have been exhibited in galleries beside the artworks that inspired them.

"Grandmother" was first published in *Threads & Dust* (Finishing Line Press, 2005). The poem also was published in *Necessity of Flight* (Cherry Grove, 2011).

Susan J. Anderson holds a Master's of Science in Creative Writing from Towson University, and is an award-winning teacher of English and creative writing. She writes poetry, fiction and nonfiction, and blogs at foxywriterchick.com. Susan lives in Maryland with her husband and three sons.

Lana Hechtman Ayers is a poet, novelist, publisher, and time-travel enthusiast. She facilitates generative writing workshops, leads salons for book groups, and teaches at writers' conferences. Lana resides in coastal Oregon where she enjoys the near-constant plink of rain on the roof and the sea's steady whoosh. She is obsessed with exotic ice cream flavors, Little Red Riding Hood, and monochromatic cats and dogs. Her favorite color is the swirl of Van Gogh's *Starry Night*.

"Red Riding Hood Remembers Grandma" appears in Lana's collection *Red Riding Hood's Real Life: a novel in verse* (Night Rain Press, 2017).

Judy Barrat was for most of her life what she calls a "closet writer" of poetry and short fiction until a friend convinced to bring her words into the light. She has since shared her words at poetry and music venues around Los Angeles and has had her work published in several magazines and anthologies and has performed two very successful one-woman shows of her poetry and stories, with musical accompaniment, at a Hollywood supper club.

Judith Barrington has published four poetry collections, most recently *The Conversation* (Salmon Poetry) and two chapbooks: *Postcard from the Bottom*

of the Sea and *Lost Lands* (winner of the Robin Becker
Chapbook Award). Her *New and Selected* will come out
in early 2018 from Salmon Press. She lives in Oregon
and has been a faculty member of the MFA Program
at the University of Alaska, Anchorage. More at: www.
judithbarrington.com

Ellen Bass's most recent book is *Like a Beggar* (Copper
Canyon Press, 2014). Her poetry frequently appears in
The New Yorker, The American Poetry Review, and many
other journals. Among her awards are Fellowships from
the National Endowment for the Arts and the California
Arts Council, three Pushcart Prizes, and The Lambda
Literary Award. A Chancellor of the Academy of American
Poets, she teaches in the MFA writing program at Pacific
University. www.ellenbass.com

"Reincarnation" was previously published in *The New
Yorker.*

Anthony Beal is a WSET-3 wine scholar and the creator
of the food, wine, and spirits blog FlavorfulWorld.com. He
is also a comic book geek, aspiring gym rat, and member
of the Wine Scholar Guild and the Society of Wine
Educators. When not writing about tasty things he has
drunk, he enjoys traveling, studying Japanese language
and culture, and being a devoted father and husband.

"Little Apples of Sanlúcar" was first published with
VintageWinePoems.com.

"Maenad" was first published with VintageWinePoems.com.

Sheila Bender's most recent poetry collection is *Behind Us the Way Grows Wider*. Her many books on writing include the newly reprinted instructional volumes *Writing in a Convertible with the Top Down* and *Writing Personal Essays: Shaping and Sharing Your Life Experience*. Her prose memoir, *A New Theology: Turning to Poetry in a Time of Grief* continues to help others who are suffering loss. She is the founder of WritingItReal.com, a website dedicated to facilitating those who write from personal experience, no matter the genre.

"At Snowfall" appears in *Behind Us the Way Grows Wider: Collected Poems 1980–2013*.

Kenneth Bennight resides in San Antonio, Texas. He is a husband, father, lawyer, former Marine, native Texan, and the grandfather of the cutest little boy on the face of the Earth. Kenneth is the author of the Nacho Perez stories, hard-boiled detective fiction set in contemporary Texas, as well as other short stories and a legal reference work called *Texas Law of Streets and Alleys: A Handbook*.

Bruce Berger's poems have appeared in *The New York Times, Barron's, Orion* and numerous literary reviews, and have been collected in *Facing the Music*. He was awarded the Karen Chamberlain Lifetime Achievement Award for Poetry by the 2016 Headwaters Poetry Festival, and in 2008 he was sent by the US State Department to represent American poetry at a conference in northern India, followed by readings in New Delhi and Mumbai.

Jane Blanchard lives and writes in Georgia. Her work has appeared in journals, magazines, and anthologies around the world. She has published two collections, *Unloosed*

(2016) and *Tides & Currents* (2017), both through Kelsay Books.

"Uncorked" previously appeared in *RiverSedge.*

Rachel Squires Bloom's poems have appeared in *Hawaii Review, Poet Lore, Fugue, Main Street Rag, Kimera, Poetry East, Nomad's Choir, Mad Poet's Review, Bluster, 96 Inc., Bellowing Ark, Slugfest, Thin Air, Taproot Literary Review, True Romance, Lucid Stone, Green Hills Literary Lantern, California Quarterly, Chest,* and *Mudfish.* Her book, *A Great Place to Start: History of the Squantum School,* was published in 2016. She teaches in Quincy, Massachusetts.

Anita K. Boyle is an artist and poet just outside Bellingham, WA, at Egress Studio. She also publishes handmade limited-edition books by the poets of Washington State. Her own publications include the books *What the Alder Told Me, The Drenched, Bamboo Equals Loon.* Boyle has participated in several collaborative publications with her poet-partner James Bertolino—most written in noisy brew pubs or beside the Noon Road Pond, all while enjoying brightly bitter IPAs. *Prost!*

Allen Braden's work has appeared in: *City of the Big Shoulders: An Anthology of Chicago Poetry; In Their Cups: An Anthology of Poems about Drinking Places, Drinks, and Drinkers; The Liberal Media Made Me Do It: Poetic Responses to NPR & PBS Stories* and *The World Is Charged: Poetic Engagements with Gerard Manley Hopkins.* Assistant poetry editor of *Terrain.org: A Journal of the Built + Natural Environments,* he lives in Lakewood, Washington.

"Both Portraits" was previously published in *Elegy in the Passive Voice* (University of Alaska/Fairbanks).

Jerry Bradley, a member of the Texas Institute of Letters, is Professor of English at Lamar University and the author of 7 books. His poems have appeared in *New England Review, Modern Poetry Studies,* and *Southern Humanities Review.* Poetry editor of *Concho River Review,* Bradley won the 2015 Boswell Poetry Prize, and he is past-president of the Texas Association of Creative Writing Teachers. The Southwest Popular Culture Association endows a writing award in his name.

"If You're Drinking to Forget, Please Pay in Advance" was originally published in *New Texas,* 2009, and then appeared in Bradley's collection *Crownfeathers and Effigies* (Lamar University Press, 2014).

Shirley J. Brewer graduated from careers in bartending, palm-reading and speech therapy. She serves as poet-in-residence at Carver Center for the Arts & Technology in Baltimore. Her poems garnish *Barrow Street, Poetry East, Slant, Gargoyle, Comstock Review,* and many other journals. Shirley's poetry chapbooks include *A Little Breast Music* (Passager Books, 2008) and *After Words* (Apprentice House, 2013). In 2017, Main Street Rag released her first full-length collection of poems, *Bistro in Another Realm.*

Liz Bruno is a doctoral candidate in English at the University of Oregon. She currently lives in midcoast Maine with her daughter and works at an outdoor school. She is finishing her dissertation on early 20th century literature and educational theory. In 2017, she was awarded a Peter K. Hixson prize in poetry.

"Drink" was previously published in *Roast Magazine*. It was also the winner of the 2009 Davis Demitasse Poetry Competition.

Cale Budweiser is a poet of alcoholic beverages, wine, beer and spirits, Dio-nietzschean rather than Apollon-arian.

Jennifer Bullis is author of the chapbook *Impossible Lessons* (MoonPath Press). Her poems appear in *Water~Stone Review, Tinderbox, Iron Horse, Bellingham Review, Heavy Feather, Muse /A Journal,* and *Tahoma.* She is recipient of an Honorable Mention in the 2017 Gulf Coast Prize for Nonfiction. Originally from Reno, Nevada, she holds a Ph.D. in English from the University of California Davis and lives in Bellingham, Washington, where she taught college writing and literature for 14 years.

Rosalie Calabrese is a native New Yorker and management consultant for the arts whose poems have appeared in publications ranging from *And Then* to *Cosmopolitan, Jewish Currents* to *Poetry New Zealand,* as well as *The New York Times* and other newspapers, anthologies (including the *1997 Anthology of Magazine Verse & Yearbook of American Poetry*), and on the Web. Her most recent book, *Remembering Chris,* is published by Poets Wear Prada.

Jeremy Cantor began writing after retiring from a career in laboratory chemistry. He was a finalist for the Lascaux Prize in Poetry for his debut collection *Wisteria from Seed* (Kelsay Books, 2015) and a semi-finalist for the Dartmouth Poet in Residence at the Frost Place in

New Hampshire. A set of his poems is forthcoming in *Interdisciplinary Studies in Literature and the Environment* (*ISLE*, published in conjunction with Oxford University Press).

"Lengthwise" appeared in his collection *Wisteria from Seed* (Alabaster Leaves Publishing, an imprint of Kelsay Books, 2015).

Nancy Canyon, MFA, developed a taste for wine when her father carried home gallon jugs of handmade Chianti from the restaurant located next to his office in Spokane. The taste, of course, was inferior to the wine she later savored in Tuscany. Now she prefers sipping an oaky red by the fire. Nancy's a writer and painter, and is widely published: *Raven Chronicles, Tishman Review, Water~Stone Review, Floating Bridge Press, Clover*, and more. www.nancycanyon.com

Neil Carpathios is the author of five full-length poetry collections, most recently *Confessions of a Captured Angel* (Terrapin Books, 2016) and *Far Out Factoids* (FutureCycle Press, 2017).
"Drowning My Sorrows" originally appeared in *Beyond the Bones* (FutureCycle Press, 2009). He teaches at Shawnee State University in Portsmouth, Ohio.

Patricia Carragon loves cats, chocolate, haiku, and Brooklyn. Her latest book is *Innocence* (Finishing Line Press, 2017). *The Cupcake Chronicles* is forthcoming from Poets Wear Prada. Patricia is an active member of Brevitas, PEN Women's Literary Workshop, Women Writers in Bloom, and Tamarind. She is an executive editor for *Home Planet News Online*.

DeWitt Clinton is Emeritus Professor at the University of Wisconsin—Whitewater, and lives in Shorewood, Wisconsin. He continues to write and publish short creative non-fiction and poetry in *Wise Guys: An Online Magazine, Negative Capability, Cha: An Asian Literary Journal, Verse-Virtual, New Verse News, Peacock Journal, Ekphrasic Review* and *Stark: The Poetry Journal No. 1* which featured a "shortlisted" poem for the Wisehouse International Poetry Award.

Brian Cooney grew up in New York and now lives in Spokane, WA, where he teaches literature at Gonzaga University. Inspired by Juvenal, Brian began writing poetry a few years ago. His works have been published in journals such as *Hotel Amerika, Lumina, Pacifica Literary Review,* and *Parcel,* and his chapbooks *The Descent of Ham* (alice blue) and *My Idea of Fun* (Floating Bridge) both came out in 2015.

Barbara Lydecker Crane is the author of two chapbooks: *Zero Gravitas* (White Violet Press, 2012) and *Alphabetricks* (for children, Daffydowndilly Books, 2013). She won the 2011 Helen Schaible International Sonnet Contest. Her poems have appeared or are forthcoming in *American Arts Quarterly, Angle, Atlanta Review, First Things, The Flea, Light Quarterly, Magma Poetry, Measure, Snakeskin,* and *14 by 14,* among others, and in eight anthologies.

"Finding Rumi in a Wine Bar" was previously published in the online poetry journal *The Ghazal Page* in June, 2015.

Mary Eliza Crane is a northwest poet residing in the Cascade foothills. A regular feature at poetry venues in the Puget Sound region, she has read poetry from Woodstock to LA. Mary has two volumes of poetry, *What I Can Hold In My Hands* and *At First Light*, both published by Gazoobi Tales. Her work has appeared in journals including *Raven Chronicles, Cartier Street Review, Tuesday Poem* and others, and several anthologies.

"My Father's Sweater" appeared in *At First Light* (Gazoobi Tales Publishing, 2011).

Jackie Craven is the author of *Secret Formulas & Techniques of the Masters* (Brick Road Poetry Press, 2018). Her poetry has appeared in *Columbia Poetry Review, New Ohio Review, Nimrod, River Styx, Spillway*, and many other journals. Omnidawn selected her chapbook, *Our Lives Became Unmanageable*, for their Fabulist Fiction award. Find her at www.JackieCraven.com.

"Thirst" appears in *Secret Formulas & Techniques of the Masters* (Brick Road Poetry Press, 2018).

Michelle Cristiani teaches reading and writing at Portland Community College. She earned a Ph.D. in anthropology in 2003 from the University of New Mexico. Michelle placed in two categories in the Oregon Poetry Association's spring 2015 contest. She will also be published this summer in *Awakenings Review*. She has been published in *Reality Mom Zine, Poetry Theater Press*, and *Conceptions Southwest*. Michelle lives in Portland, Oregon.

Barbara Crooker is the author of eight books of poetry; *Les Fauves* is the most recent. Her work has appeared in a variety of literary journals, including *Common Wealth: Contemporary Poets on Pennsylvania* and

The Bedford Introduction to Literature. She has received a number of awards, including the 2004 WB Yeats Society of New York Award, the 2003 Thomas Merton Poetry of the Sacred Award, and three Pennsylvania Council on the Arts Creative Writing Fellowships.

"Martini" was first published in *Gargoyle.*

"The Wine Tasting" was published in *Barbara Crooker: Selected Poems* (FutureCycle Press, 2015).

John Davis is the author of two collections, *Gigs* and *The Reservist.* His work has appeared in *Cutbank, DMQ Review, Iron Horse Literary Review, One* and *Rio Grande Review.* He lives on an island west of Seattle, teaches writing and performs in blues bands.

William Derge's poems have appeared in *Negative Capability, The Bridge, Artful Dodge, Bellingham Review,* and many other publications. He is the winner of the $1000 2010 Knightsbridge Prize judged by Donald Hall and nominated for a Pushcart Prize. He is a winner of the Rainmaker Award judged by Marge Piercy. He has received honorable mentions in contests sponsored by *The Bridge, Sow's Ear,* and *New Millennium,* among others. He has been awarded a grant by the Maryland State Arts Council.

Patrick Dixon is a writer/photographer retired from careers in teaching and commercial fishing. Published in *Cirque Literary Journal, Panoplyzine, Raven Chronicles,* and the anthologies *FISH* 2015 and *WA129,* he is the poetry editor of *National Fisherman* magazine's quarterly, *North Pacific Focus.* Patrick received an Artist Trust Grant for Artists to edit *Anchored in Deep*

Water: The FisherPoets Anthology published in 2014. His chapbook *Arc of Visibility* won the 2015 Alabama State Poetry Morris Memorial Award.

Victoria Doerper is a writer of memoir, non-fiction, and poetry. Her poetry appears in *Noisy Water: Poetry from Whatcom County, Washington; Clover; and Cirque.* Her prose appears in *Orion Magazine.* Her husband, John Doerper, is the author of travel guides to the wine country of California, Washington, and Oregon; she happily tippled sips of his uncorked research subjects. In her memoir she writes of her husband's garden, where grape vines twine through the trees.

Mark Donnelly is a writer of poetry, plays and short stories, with numerous publication credits. He has an M.F.A. in Creative Writing from Brooklyn College of the City University of New York and teaches English at St. Francis College in Brooklyn Heights and Borough of Manhattan Community College. He is a member of the Dramatists Guild of America, Irish American Writers and Artists, and Artists Without Walls. He lives in Queens, New York.

Katherine Edgren's book of poetry, *The Grain Beneath the Gloss,* was recently published by Finishing Line Press. Her two chapbooks: *Long Division* (2014) and *Transports* (2009) were also published by them. Her poems have appeared in *Christian Science Monitor, Birmingham Poetry Review* and *Barbaric Yawp,* among others. She was born in 1950 and is a retired social worker, mother and grandmother, and lives in Dexter, Michigan with her husband and her dog.

Bryce Emley is a freelancer, editor, and barista in New Mexico. His poetry and prose can be found in *The Atlantic, Narrative, Boston Review, Prairie Schooner, Best American Experimental Writing*, etc., and he serves as Poetry Editor of *Raleigh Review*. Read more at bryceemley.com.

"College Beer" was previously published in an earlier form on sixfold.org, Winter 2014: https://www.sixfold. org/PoWinter14/Emley.html.

Susan J. Erickson's first full-length collection of poems, *Lauren Bacall Shares a Limousine*, won the Brick Road Poetry Prize. Her work appears in *Crab Creek Review, Sliver of Stone, The Fourth River* and *The Tishman Review*. Susan lives in Bellingham, Washington, where she helped establish the Sue C. Boynton Poetry Walk and Contest. You can learn more about her writing at www. susanjerickson.com.

Timons Esaias is the author of the collection *Why Elephants No Longer Communicate in Greek*. His works— including short fiction, essays, and satires—have appeared in 20 languages. His poetry publications include *Atlanta Review, Verse Daily, 5AM, Pittsburgh Poetry Review, Willard & Maple, Asimov's Science Fiction,* and *Elysian Fields Quarterly: The Literary Journal of Baseball*. His short story "Sadness" was selected for three Year's Best anthologies in 2015. He lives in Pittsburgh.

"The Alcoholic Beverages of India" first appeared in the collection *Why Elephants No Longer Communicate in Greek*, (Concrete Wolf Press, 2016).

A Seattle native, **Sheila Farr** participates in the Northwest's cultural scene as a poet, author, and journalist. Her poetry has appeared in *American Literary Review*, the *New York Quarterly*, and *Seattle Review*, among others. Her books include monographs on the artists Fay Jones, Leo Kenney, James Martin, and Richard C. Elliott. From 2000—2009, she served as staff visual arts critic for *The Seattle Times*.

Brian C. Felder is a veteran of both the Vietnam War and the American poetry scene and can honestly say that the latter holds as many booby traps as the former. Though he's been rejected more times than he can count, his work has been published in magazines coast-to-coast, including *Perceptions, Big Muddy, Art:Mag, Chiron Review, Askew, Atlanta Review, Iconoclast, Ship of Fools, Plainsongs, Connecticut River Review* and, most notably, *The Humanist.*

"Evening Solace" previously appeared in *ART:MAG #44*.

Paul Fisher's poems have appeared in journals such as *The Antioch Review, Cave Wall, Crab Creek Review, Cutthroat, Nimrod, Switched-on Gutenberg,* and in the best-selling anthology, *River of Earth and Sky: Poems for the 21st Century.* His first book, *Rumors of Shore*, won the Blue Light Book Award. His second, *An Exaltation of Tongues*, was published by MoonPath Press. Paul lives in Seattle with his wife, Linda, two bossy cats, and a five-pound poodle.

Gretchen Fletcher's poetry and travel articles have been published in numerous magazines, newspapers, journals and anthologies. She won the Poetry Society of America's Bright Lights, Big Verse competition and was projected on the Jumbotron as she read her poem in Times Square. She leads writing workshops for Florida Center for the Book, an affiliate of the Library of Congress. Her chapbooks, *That Severed Cord* and *The Scent of Oranges*, were published by Finishing Line Press.

"Just a Taste of Friendship" was published in *Wine, Cheese, and Chocolate* by Manzanita Writers Press.

"Fear of the Dark" is included in her chapbook, *The Scent of Oranges; poems from the tropics*, published by Finishing Line Press.

Alice B. Fogel is the Poet Laureate of NH (2014—2019). In addition to *Strange Terrain*, a reader's guide to appreciating poetry without necessarily "getting" it, she is a 9-time Pushcart nominee, & author of *A Doubtful House* (2017), *Interval: Poems Based on Bach's Goldberg Variations* (2015), which won the Nicholas Schaffner Award for Music in Literature & the New Hampshire Literary Award in Poetry, & *Be That Empty*, a national bestseller.

Jerome Gagnon lives in Northern California where he has worked as a teacher, tutor, and freelance journalist. He attended San Francisco State University, receiving an M.A. in English/Creative Writing. His poems have appeared recently in *Spiritus*, *Archaeopteryx*, *Poet Lore*, *Roaring Muse*, *Reed Magazine*, and several anthologies, including the just-released *Awake in the World*, published by Riverfeet Press. A chapbook, *Spell of the Ordinary*, is forthcoming from Finishing Line Press.

Two series of **Katherine Gekker**'s poems have been set to music. "...to Cast a Shadow Again" and "Chasing the Moon Down" are available on CD and iTunes. Other poems have been published, or are forthcoming, in

Little Patuxent Review, Broadkill Review, Panoply, Northern Virginia Review, and other journals. Her first book of poetry will be published by Glass Lyre Press in 2019.

James A. Gollata is a minimalist poet and word warrior. He lives outside New York City (on the east coast of Wisconsin) near the Lake Michigan shore. Major influences are Monk and Kerouac, though his style belies these guys. He wrote "In Vino Triage" for this anthology, built upward from the final movie and TV line, which he happened to exclaim at an appropriate vino moment many years ago. Veritas.

Carol Gordon is a retired Mental Health counselor living in the Upper Left Hand Corner of the country. She is active with a Continuing Education program of Edmonds Community College. She enjoys reading, traveling, and getting the occasional piece of writing done inside our perpetual *Partly Cloudy.*

"A Week After Our Daughter's Wedding We Call a Plumber" has appeared on the website of the Judson Hills Winery.

Melissa Grossman is a member of Paradigm Poets in Los Angeles, CA. Her poetry has been published in several journals, among them: *Common Ground Review, Askew,* and two Lucid Moose anthologies: *Alleyways & Gutters: Poverty & Struggle* and *Like a Girl.* In Spring 2017 Finishing Line Press published her chapbook *Through My Eyes.* She is a stained glass and mosaic artist, and lives in Simi Valley with her Golden Retriever, Molly.

John Guzlowski's writing appears in Garrison Keillor's *Writer's Almanac, North American Review, Salon.*

Com, Rattle, Nimrod, and many other print and online journals here and abroad. His writing about his parents' experiences as slave laborers in Nazi Germany and refugees in America appears in his memoir in prose and poetry, *Echoes of Tattered Tongues* (Aquila Polonica Press). Of Guzlowski's writing, Nobel Laureate Czeslaw Milosz said, "He has an astonishing ability for grasping reality."

"Talking Drunk to a Drunk Woman I Don't Know" originally appeared in the Spring 2017 issue of the *Atticus Review.*

A Pushcart Prize nominee, **Jennifer Hambrick** is the author of *Unscathed* (NightBallet Press). Her poetry has been published in dozens of literary journals and anthologies worldwide, including the *Santa Clara Review, Third Wednesday, Mad River Review,* and *Modern Haiku,* has been translated into five languages, and has won prizes in numerous international competitions. A classical singer and public radio broadcaster, Jennifer Hambrick lives in Columbus, Ohio. Her blog, *Inner Voices,* is at jenniferhambrick.com.
"Booze Run" was first published in *Haibun Today,* Vol. 10, No. 4, Dec. 2016.

Tamra J. Higgins holds an MFA from the Stonecoast Writing Program, University of Southern Maine and an M.Ed. from Northern Vermont University, Johnson, Vermont. After teaching in Vermont's public schools for 20 years, she founded Sundog Poetry Center, a nonprofit organization committed to supporting poets and sharing poetry throughout Vermont. She is the author of *Nothing Saved Us: Poems of the Korean War* and the chapbook, *Tenderbellied.*

"At the Pub" first appeared in the blog "The Quality of Light" at tamrajhiggins.com.

Lynn Hoffman, Ph.D. is a cultural anthropologist, chef, and writer who founded the Culinary Arts program at Drexel University. He is the author of the *Short Courses in Beer, Wine and Rum* series, *The Bachelor's Cat* and *Bang-Bang*, an urban novel. A Pushcart nominee, Hoffman's collection *Philadelphia Poems* was published last year by Kelsay Press.

"Drinking Song for Poets" was published in *Main Street Rag*.

Stephen Hollaway is a pastor living on the small Island of Block Island, 13 miles off the coast of Rhode Island. This poem was written as a Valentine to his wife of 38 years. He is a graduate of Princeton and Duke and has been writing poems all his life. Only now in his idyllic pre-retirement existence is he making time to submit them for publication.

"Aged Together" first appeared in *The Block Island Times*, February 14, 2014.

Steve Hood is an attorney who has lived and worked all over the U.S., and now lives in Bellingham, WA. He has a bachelor's degree in Creative Writing from Western Washington University. He has published over 50 poems and a poetry chapbook, *From Here to Astronomy*. Three of his poems won an award from the Pacific NW Writers Association. He is a political activist and has also published news articles and editorials.

Paul Hostovsky is the author of nine books of poetry, most recently *Is That What That Is* (FutureCycle Press, 2017). His poems have won a Pushcart Prize, two Best of the Net awards, and have been featured on Poetry Daily, Verse Daily, and The Writer's Almanac. More at paulhostovsky.com.

"The Debate at Duffy's" is from *A Little In Love A Lot*, by Paul Hostovsky (Main Street Rag, 2011).

Kake Huck is a desultory poet living in Central Oregon where she prefers playing to writing. Her poems have been published in small journals and anthologies, including *Regrets Only* and *Beyond Forgetting*. Her self-published novel-in-poems about mid-Century, bisexual, wife-killer Wayne Lonergan—*Murderous Glamour*—is available on Amazon.

"Pinecones, Venice" is from the collection *Sentenced to Venice*, now seeking a publisher.

Seattle's **Paul Hunter** has been poet, teacher, performer, playwright, musician, instrument-maker, artist, editor, publisher, grassroots arts activist, and shade-tree mechanic. For the past eleven years his imprint Wood Works has produced fine letterpress books. His poems have appeared in numerous journals, three full-length books, and several chapbooks. His collection of farming poems, *Breaking Ground* (Silverfish Review Press) was reviewed in the *New York Times*. A second volume of farming poems, *Ripening*, is due next year.

"Pick" was first published in *Spoon River Poetry Review*, and appeared in *Come the Harvest* (Silverfish Review Press, 2008).

Sibyl James is the author of eleven books—poetry, fiction, and travel memoirs—most recently *The Grand Piano Range* (Black Heron Press). She has taught at colleges in the U.S., China, Mexico, and—as Fulbright professor—Tunisia and Cote d'Ivoire. Her writing has received awards from Artist Trust and the Seattle, King County, and Washington State arts commissions.

"Twisp, Washington" previously appeared in the magazines *The Arts, Tendril, Pudding*, and the book *The Grand Piano Range*.

Joan Wiese Johannes has been published in journals and anthologies and has four chapbooks, including *He Thought the Periodic Table Was a Portrait of God* (Parallel Press). Her crown of sonnets *Happily Ever After* was whimsically illustrated by her poet/artist husband Jeffrey. Joan agrees with *Our Town*'s stage manager, who muses that only poets and saints truly appreciate life while living it. Although not a candidate for sainthood, she lives a good life in Port Edwards, WI.

"Happy New Year" first appeared in the *2008 Wisconsin Poets' Calendar*.

Hope Jordan's poems and stories have recently appeared or are forthcoming in *Comstock Review, Flash Flash Click, Naugatuck River Review, SLAB Literary Magazine*, and *Red Headed Stepchild*. She was the first official poetry slam master in New Hampshire. Her first chapbook, *The Day She Decided to Feed Crows*, will be published in 2017 by Cervena Barva Press. She is a member UMass Boston's Class of 2020 MFA Program in fiction.

Mary Christine Kane lives in St. Paul, Minnesota where she is a freelance writer. Her work has appeared has appeared in *Burner Magazine, OVS Magazine, Sleet, Right Here Right Now, The Buffalo Anthology, Portage Magazine, Bluestem,* and others. She earned an MFA from Hamline University.

When not concentrating upon the similarities between dew drops and condensation over surfaces warm and cold, **Sneha Subramanian Kanta** conjures philosophical axioms. A GREAT scholarship awardee, she is pursuing her second postgraduate degree in literature in England. Areas of research interest include the gaze of otherness and postcolonial theory. Her award-winning poem "At Dusk with the Gods" won the Alfaaz (Kalaage) prize. She loves the musk of whiskey and it reminds her of autumn.

Meg Kearney is author of two books of poems for adults, *An Unkindness of Ravens* and *Home By Now,* winner of the 2010 PEN New England L.L. Winship Award; as well as a trilogy of novels in verse for teens, most recently *When You Never Said Goodbye.* Meg's award-winning picture book, *Trouper,* is illustrated by E.B. Lewis. She directs the Solstice MFA Program at Pine Manor College in Massachusetts. For more information www.megkearney.com.

Susan Kelly-DeWitt is the author of *Spider Season* (Cold River Press, 2016), *The Fortunate Islands* (Marick Press, 2008), and nine previous small press collections and online chapbooks. Her work has also appeared in many anthologies, and in print and online journals at home and abroad. She is currently a member of the National

Book Critics Circle and the Northern California Book Reviewers Association. For more information, please visit her website at www.susankelly-dewitt.com.

Rick Kempa lives in Rock Springs, Wyoming, where he teaches at Western Wyoming College. His most recent books are the anthologies *On Foot: Grand Canyon Backpacking Stories*, published in 2014 by Vishnu Temple Press in Flagstaff, *GOING DOWN GRAND: Poems From The Canyon* (Lithic Press, 2015), which he co-edited with Peter Anderson, and a poetry collection *Ten Thousand Voices*, published by Littoral Press in Richmond, CA. www.rickkempa.com

A Pushcart nominee and winner of the 2016 Ken Warfel Fellowship, **J.I. Kleinberg** is co-editor of *Noisy Water: Poetry from Whatcom County, Washington* (Other Mind Press, 2015). Her poetry has appeared recently in *One, Diagram, Otoliths, Poetry Breakfast*, and elsewhere. She lives in Bellingham, Washington, and blogs most days at chocolateisaverb.wordpress.com and thepoetrydepartment.wordpress.com.

Kateri Kosek's poetry and essays have appeared in *Orion, Creative Nonfiction, Terrain, Profane,* and other journals. She teaches college English and writes for various newspapers near her home in western Massachusetts. She holds an MFA from Western Connecticut State University, where she also mentors in the MFA program. Kateri has been a resident at the Kimmel Harding Nelson Center for the Arts in Nebraska and is working on a books of essays about birds. **Avra Kouffman** is a poet, journalist, and writer of creative nonfiction. She was born and raised in New

York City and now lives in California. Avra has traveled widely and taught in the USA, Europe and Brazil. She has a doctorate in 17th and 18th century literature with a specialty in women's diaries.

John Krumberger has published a volume of poems entitled *The Language Of Rain And Wind* (Backwaters Press, 2008), and a chapbook, *In A Jar Somewhere* (Black Dirt Press, 1999). His latest collection of poems *Because Autumn* was published by Main Street Rag Press in 2016. He has a PHD in psychology from the University of Minnesota, works as a psychologist in private practice in St. Paul, MN, and lives with his wife in Minneapolis.

David M. Laws is a (mostly) retired musical instrument repair technician living in Bellingham, Washington. He graduated in 2005 from Western Washington University with a degree in English— Creative Writing Emphasis, and has never been quite the same since. He is trying very hard to stay out of trouble, but current political conditions make that difficult. He only drinks occasionally now (mostly due to current political conditions).

Shannon P. Laws, born Seattle WA, lives ninety miles north in Bellingham where she was honored with a Mayor's Arts Award in 2013. She also received a Community Champion Award courtesy of the Writer's International Network in Richmond, B.C., Canada. Shannon's latest project is Poem Booth, a collaboration with painter Christen Mattix and poet Summer Starr. The project reclaims derelict phone booths, transforming them into creative points of communication and poetry rotated every quarter.

"Rancid Blood" appeared in *Odd Little Things* (Chickadee Productions, 2014).

John Leighton lives on Teal Lake in northwestern Wisconsin. His home points directly east to Paradise Island where throughout the seasons he watches the sun track Paradise end to end. He published a book of poems *Paradise View, Collected Poems* in 2013. John is retired, and spends much of his time as a volunteer.

Jared Leising grew up in the Midwest, and is the author of a chapbook—*The Widows and Orphans of Winesburg, Ohio*. Before moving to Seattle, he received his M.F.A. in Creative Writing from the University of Houston. In 2000 Jared began teaching English at Cascadia College, and in 2010, he curated the Jack Straw Writers Program. This year, he's begun teaching a creative writing class for women at the King County Jail.

"The Beer Ted Kooser Owes Us All" was previously published online at Poet's Musings: http:// poetsmusings-muser.blogspot.com/2007/10/guest-poet-jared-leising-on-beer-ted.html.

Brenna Lemieux has published two collections of poetry, *The Gospel of Household Plants* and *Blankness, Melancholy, and Other Ways of Dying*. She lives in Chicago.

Thomas Lequin is a priest, farmer, Maine Master Guide, hunter and fisherman. His poems have appeared in *Plough, Anglican Theological Review, The Alembic, Iodine Poetry Journal, Iconoclast*, an anthology, *The Wildest Peal, Contemporary Animal Poetry II* (Moon Pie Press, 2015), and in many other literary journals. He lives in Maine.

Sara Levinson was born in Greensburg, PA and works in the software industry in California. Her writing has appeared in the *Pittsburgh Post-Gazette*, the *American Scholar*, *The Gettysburg Times*, *Thrive Global,* and *Ruminate* magazine. She is also an accomplished musician. Sara holds a master's degree in professional writing from Carnegie Mellon University in Pittsburgh and an undergraduate degree in English Literature from Gettysburg College. She lives in Los Angeles with her husband, Drew.

David Lloyd is the author of nine books, including three poetry collections: *Warriors* (Salt Publishing, 2012), *The Gospel According to Frank* (New American Press, 2009), and *The Everyday Apocalypse* (Three Conditions Press, 2002). In 2000, he received the Poetry Society of America's Robert H. Winner Memorial Award. His poems have appeared in numerous magazines including *Crab Orchard Review, DoubleTake,* and *Planet.* He directs the Creative Writing Program at Le Moyne College in Syracuse, NY.

Ellaraine Lockie is a widely published and awarded poet, nonfiction book author and essayist. She has published thirteen chapbook collections of poetry. Collections have won the Encircle Publications Chapbook Contest, Poetry Forum's Chapbook Contest Prize, San Gabriel Valley Poetry Festival Chapbook Contest, the Aurorean's Chapbook Choice Award, and Best Individual Collection Award from *Purple Patch* magazine in England. Ellaraine teaches poetry workshops and serves as Poetry Editor for the lifestyles magazine, *Lilipoh.*

"Dinner Date" was previously published by *Casa de Cinco Hermanas*.

Amy Locklin has edited two print fiction anthologies and published a print chapbook of poetry entitled *The Secondary Burial*.

Amy MacLennan has been published in *Hayden's Ferry Review, River Styx, Linebreak, Cimarron Review, The Pedestal*, and *Rattle*. Her chapbook, *The Fragile Day*, was released from Spire Press, and her chapbook, *Weathering*, was published by Uttered Chaos Press. Her full-length collection, *The Body, A Tree*, was published by MoonPath Press in 2016.

Susan Mahan has been writing poetry since her husband died in 1997. She has self-published four chapbooks, including *Missing Mum* (2005) and *World View* (2009). She has been published in numerous anthologies, including *Kiss Me Goodnight, Solace in So Many Words, Living Lessons, Crave It: Writers and Artists Do Food, Cradle Songs: An Anthology About Motherhood*, and most recently *The Widows' Handbook*. Her work has been included in poetry exhibits in Boston City Hall.

Brandon Marlon is a writer from Ottawa, Canada. He received his B.A. in Drama & English from the University of Toronto and his M.A. in English from the University of Victoria. His poetry was awarded the Harry Hoyt Lacey Prize in Poetry (Fall 2015), and his writing has been published in 175+ publications in 23 countries. www.brandonmarlon.com.

Tod Marshall, born in Buffalo, New York, grew up in Wichita, Kansas. He holds a PhD from The University of Kansas. He directs the writing concentration and coordinates visiting writers at Gonzaga University where he is the Robert K. and Ann J. Powers Endowed Professor in the Humanities. He enjoys backpacking and fishing and spends about a month of every year in a tent. From 2016-2018, he will serve as the Washington State Poet Laureate.

Marsha Mathews's new chapbook, *Growing Up with Pigtails,* presents both narrative and lyrical reflections on that sometimes troubling, sometimes triumphant experience of growing up, girl. Earlier books include *Hallelujah Voices* (Aldrich, 2012), *Sunglow & a Tuft of Nottingham Lace,* (Red Berry Editions), and *Northbound Single-Lane,* (Finishing Line, 2010). Her work appears in *Appalachian Heritage, Delmarva Review, The Los Angeles Review, Potomac Review,* and other fine publications.

"Stuck" was first published in *The Muse: An International Journal of Poetry.* Ed. Pradeep Chaswal. December 2013.

Andrew Shattuck McBride is a writer with work in *Perfume River Poetry Review, Cirque: A Literary Journal for the North Pacific Rim, The Last Walk: Using Poetry for Grieving and Remembering Our Pets, Acorn, Cooweescoowee, Raven Chronicles,* and *Clover, A Literary Rag.* He edits historical novels, memoirs, poetry collections and chapbooks. When he's not writing or editing, he herds his (inside only) cat Angel. www.andrewsmcbride. wordpress.com

Kathleen McClung, author of *Almost the Rowboat,* has work in *Mezzo Cammin, Unsplendid, Peacock Journal, Forgotten Women, Raising Lilly Ledbetter: Women Poets*

Occupy the Workspace, and elsewhere. Winner of the Rita Dove, Maria W. Faust, and Shirley Mcclure poetry prizes, Mcclung judges sonnets for the Soul-Making Keats literary competition and reviews books for the William Saroyan International Prize for Writing. She lives in San Francisco and teaches at Skyline College and the Writing Salon. www.kathleenmcclung.com

Jacob Minasian received his MFA in poetry from Saint Mary's College of California, where he was the 2016 Academy of American Poets University and College Poetry Prize winner, and was awarded two MFA Advisory Board Fellowships. He was also a 2012-13 Ina Coolbrith Memorial Poetry Prize winner, placing 3rd overall. His work has appeared in *Poets.org, Gyroscope Review,* and *Causeway Lit,* among others. He currently lives in Cincinnati, Ohio.

Derek Mong is the author of two poetry collections from Saturnalia Books, *Other Romes* (2011) and *The Identity Thief* (2018), and a chapbook from Two Sylvias Press, *The Ego and the Empiricist* (2017). His poetry, translations, and essays have appeared in *Two Lines,* the *Kenyon Review, Blackbird, Pleiades,* the *Gettysburg Review,* and elsewhere. He lives with his family in Indiana, where he is the Byron K. Trippet Assistant Professor of English at Wabash College.

"An Ordinary Evening in San Francisco" originally appeared online at *Blue Lyra Review* in June of 2015, issue 4.2.

John Morgan has published six books of poetry and a collection of essays. His work has appeared in *The New Yorker, Poetry, The American Poetry Review, The New*

Republic, The Paris Review, and many other magazines. Winner of the Discovery Award of the New York Poetry Center, Morgan divides his time between Fairbanks, Alaska, and Bellingham, Washington. For more information visit his website: johnmorganpoet.com

"Ambush" has previously appeared in *TriQuarterly* and in John Morgan's collection *Spear-Fishing on the Chatanika: New and Selected Poems,* from Salmon Poetry.

As a child in Beaver County, Pennsylvania, **Jeff Murphy** was inspired creatively by his grandmother's poetry. He graduated with his B.S. in Physics from Youngstown State University, before meandering into Geographic Information Systems (GIS). Jeff's creativity was rekindled by the estimable organization Lit Youngstown, who is re-igniting the literary arts in Youngstown. He is married to a wonderful woman in Poland, Ohio where they raise their two children.

Jed Myers lives in Seattle. He's author of *Watching the Perseids* (Sacramento Poetry Center Book Award), *The Marriage of Space and Time* (MoonPath Press, forthcoming), and two chapbooks. Honors received include *Southern Indiana Review*'s Editors' Award, the *Prime Number Magazine* Award for Poetry, and *The Southeast Review*'s Gearhart Poetry Prize. Poems have appeared in *Rattle, Poetry Northwest, Prairie Schooner, Southern Poetry Review, Crab Orchard Review, Solstice, Canary,* and elsewhere. He's Poetry Editor for *Bracken.*

Sheila Nickerson, a former poet Laureate of Alaska, has been widely published. Her most recent full-length collection is *Hitchhiking the Highway of Tears* (MoonPath

Press, 2017). Her most recent prose title is *Harnessed to the Pole: Sledge Dogs in Service to American Explorers of the Arctic: 1853–1909* (University of Alaska Press, 2014). A graduate of the Chapin School and Bryn Mawr College, she holds a doctorate in Creative Writing from Union Institute and University.

Nancy Nowak holds an MFA from Sarah Lawrence College. Her poems have appeared in *Fireweed, Poetry Northwest, The Jefferson Monthly, Iris: A Journal about Women, The Journal of Progressive Human Services,* and *The MacGuffin,* among other publications, as well as in the anthologies *The Zeppelin Reader* and *Windblown Sheets: Poems by Mothers and Daughters.* As an associate professor at Umpqua Community College, she taught writing from 1994 to 2016. She lives in Winston, OR.

Daniel Ari says: **"Fang" O'Donnell** is my neighbor and friend. I knew him 20 years as a motorcycle repairman, urban farmer, truck driver, barista and activist, while often hearing about other past pursuits (exhibition fighting, radio talent, lobster fishing, etc.) before he ever showed me his poems. Since he doesn't pursue publication, I've taken to circulating his poetry along with my own. It's satisfying, at least for me, when Fang reaches new audiences.

Leah O'Sullivan has had prose and poetry works published in *CrossCurrents Literary & Arts Magazine, Wetlands Magazine, SPANK the CARP, Route 7 Review, Mackenzie Publishing,* and *OPOSSUM,* and has received the Esther Wagner Fiction Award for her short story, "The Dying." She is currently pursuing her MFA in Creative Writing Prose at Mills College.

Richard Parisio has worked as an interpretive naturalist in the Everglades, Pocono Mountains, Assateague Island, the Catskills, and Hudson valley. He is NYS Coordinator for *River of Words,* a national children's poetry and art contest on the theme of watersheds. His collection, *The Owl Invites Your Silence,* won the 2014 Slapering Hol Press Poetry Chapbook Contest. Parisio lives in New Paltz, NY, where he is a columnist for the local paper.

Christopher Patton has published three books, among them *Ox,* a volume of poetry, and *Curious Masonry: Three Translations from the Anglo-Saxon.* Another book of translations from Old English, *Unlikeness Is Us,* was published by Gaspereau Press in late 2017. Patton's poetry has received four Pushcart Prize nominations and has appeared in *The Paris Review, Kenyon Review, Colorado Review, New American Writing,* and elsewhere. He teaches at Western Washington University and blogs at artofcompost.wordpress.com.

Robert Perchan's poetry chapbooks are *Mythic Instinct Afternoon* (2005 Poetry West Prize) and *Overdressed to Kill* (Backwaters Press 2005 Weldon Kees Award). His poetry collection *Fluid in Darkness, Frozen in Light* won the 1999 Pearl Poetry Prize. His avant-la-lettre flash novel *Perchan's Chorea: Eros and Exile* (Watermark Press, Wichita, 1991) was translated into French and published by Quidam Editeurs (Meudon) in 2002. He eats and drinks in Pusan, South Korea. Find him at robertperchan.com.

Roger Pfingston, a retired teacher of English and photography, is the recipient of a Creative Writing Fellowship from the National Endowment for the Arts and two PEN Syndicated Fiction Awards. His poems have appeared in *Rhino, American Journal of Poetry, Poet Lore, Hamilton Stone Review, Spoon River Poetry Review, Innisfree Poetry Journal, Poetry East,* and Ted Kooser's column, *American Life in Poetry.* His chapbook, *A Day Marked for Telling,* is available from Finishing Line Press.

"Grady's Imperial Pint" was published in *Sin Fronteras* #14, 2010.

Paul S. Piper was born in Chicago, lived in Montana (where he received an MFA in Creative Writing) and Hawaii, and is currently a librarian at Western Washington University. He has published six poetry collections, the most recent being *and Light.* His work has appeared in numerous anthologies. He co-edited the books *A Flutter of Birds Passing through Heaven: a tribute to Robert Sund, Father Nature* and *X-Stories: The Personal Side of Fragile X Syndrome.*

Kyle Potvin's first poetry collection, *Sound Travels on Water* (Finishing Line Press), won the 2014 Jean Pedrick Chapbook Award. She was a past finalist for the Howard Nemerov Sonnet Award. Her poems have appeared in *The New York Times, Measure, The Huffington Post, JAMA, Able Muse* and others. A member of the Powow River Poets, she is an advisor to Frost Farm Poetry in Derry, NH, and helps produce the New Hampshire Poetry Festival.

Rena Priest is a writer, poet, and performer. She is a Lummi tribal member and was raised in a subterranean homesick matriarchy. Her chapbook, *Patriarchy Blues,* was published by MoonPath Press in the summer of 2017. Rena holds an MFA in Writing from Sarah

Lawrence College and has taught various subjects in writing, contemporary American Indian issues, and literature at Northwest Indian College, Western Washington University, and Fairhaven College.

C.J. Prince of Bellingham, Washington, picks her own pockets for words, wears a shawl of metaphors, and a wide brimmed hat of grammar. Prince most recently published *Fox*, a chapbook, and is author of the poetry book *Mother, May I?*, a novel *Canvas Angels*, and *Twenty Four Houses*, a chapbook. Prince received the Distinguished Poet Award from Writers International Network Canada.

"Don't" was previously published in *Mother, May I?* by C.J. Prince, under the title "Waiting for the Red Eye."

Robert Michael Pyle is a biologist, writer, and forty-year denizen along the Lower Columbia River, where he writes poetry, fiction, essay, and scientific papers about the butterflies and the Maritime Rain Forest. Pyle's twenty-two books include the Burroughs Medal-winning *Wintergreen, Through a Green Lens: Fifty Years of Writing for Nature*, two poetry collections, and a novel, *Magdalena Mountain*. The benevolent blend of water, hops, yeast, and barley has been his pleasant companion and sometime muse.

"Duffy's Deck: 27 July 2015" was previously published in *Chinook & Chanterelle: Poems* (Lost Horse Press, 2016), and is reprinted with permission.

David Radavich has published seven poetry collections, most recently *The Countries We Live In* (2014), and co-edited a volume called *Magic Again:*

Selected Poems on Thomas Wolfe (2016). His plays have been performed across the U.S., including six Off-Off-Broadway, and in Europe. He has served as president of the Thomas Wolfe Society, Charlotte Writers Club, and North Carolina Poetry Society.

"Wine in the Ruins" appeared in *Weyfarers* (UK) and was reprinted in the author's *Greatest Hits* (Pudding House, 2000).

James Rodgers, a Northwest poet, has lived in Pacific, Washington for over 2 decades. James has three self-published chapbooks, *Ha Ha Very Funny, Love Fits*, and *Haikooky*. His first full-length manuscript, *They Were Called Records, Kids* was released in 2018 by MoonPath Press. He's had poems published in multiple publications, including a poem and photo in *Evo Magazine*, published by Duke University. James has won multiple awards, including first prize in the WPA humor category.

Mary Kay Rummel was Poet Laureate of Ventura County, California from 2014-16. Her seventh book of poetry, *The Lifeline Trembles*, won the Blue Light Poetry Prize. A new collection, *Cypher Garden*, has just been published by Blue Light Press. Her poems recently appear in *Nimrod, Askew, The Ekphrastic Review, Miramar, Pirene's Fountain*, and *AMORE: A Collection of Love Poems*. She teaches at California State University, Channel Islands, and lives in Ventura and Minneapolis. marykayrummel.com

Carly Sachs is the author of *the steam sequence* and is the editor of the anthology, *the why and later*. She writes and teaches yoga in Lexington, Kentucky.

"A Drinker's Love Poem" was previously published in *The Delaware Poetry Review.*

Florence Sage of Astoria OR has been founding organizer of Monday Mike for spoken word, poetry editor for *Hipfish* monthly, and since 1998 a co-producer of the annual FisherPoets Gathering. She currently reads at Ric's Poetry Mic, first Tuesdays in Astoria. Her 2014 collection is *Nevertheless: Poems from the Gray Area,* Hipfish Publications. She is working on a new poetry manuscript: *Menagerie.*

"Sneak, Sneaked, Snuck" first appeared in the 2016 edition of *Rain Magazine.*

Samara is a two-time Pushcart nominee whose work has appeared or is forthcoming in *Inklette, Eyedrum Periodically, Peacock Journal, Memoryhouse,* and others. She has two children, works in marketing and design, and has returned to university to complete her BA in Poetry. More at www.samarawords.com.

"Ode to a Stout" has also appeared as a video recitation on Samara's personal blog.

Rikki Santer's work has appeared in numerous publications including *Ms. Magazine, Poetry East, Margie, Crab Orchard Review, Grimm, Slipstream,* and *The Main Street Rag.* Her fifth and newest collection, *The Syntax of Trouble,* is forthcoming from NightBallet Press. She lives in Columbus, Ohio where she teaches literature, writing and film studies at a public high school. www.rikkisanter.com

"Menu" appears in Rikki Santer's collection, *Kahiki Redux*, a tribute to the late Kahiki Supper Club of Columbus, Ohio, the largest free-standing Polynesian restaurant in the U.S. for forty years.

Michael Schein wrote *John Surratt: The Lincoln Assassin Who Got Away* (2015), *Bones Beneath Our Feet: A Historical Novel of Puget Sound* (2011), and *Just Deceits: A Historical Courtroom Mystery* (2005). His altered ego, A.B. Bard, has been blamed for the poetry collection/urban fantasy, *The Killer Poet's Guide to Immortality* (2012). Michael's poetry is widely published in journals and anthologies. He is the founder of the annual LiTFUSE Poets' Workshop. More at michaelschein.com & wryink.com

Tina Schumann is the author of the poetry collections *As If* (Parlor City Press) winner of the Stephen Dunn Poetry Prize, Requiem; *A Patrimony of Fugues* (Diode) winner of the 2016 Diode Editions Chapbook Contest; and *Praising the Paradox* (Red Hen Press, 2019), finalist in the National Poetry Series and others. She is editor of *Two Countries. U.S. Daughters and Sons of Immigrant Parents* (Red Hen Press, 2017). Her poems have appeared widely since 1999. www.tinaschumann.com

"Seven Ways of Looking at a Corkscrew" previously appeared in *Raven Chronicles* and *FEAST: Poetry and Recipes for a Full Serving at the Table* (Black Lawrence Press).

Harvey Schwartz learned Americana growing up on the east coast. He unlearned it at Woodstock, a hippie commune, and during extensive hitchhiking. A long chiropractic career offered another perspective. He's been published in *Clover, Inkspeak, Jeopardy, The Kumquat Challenge, Noisy Water, Peace Poems, PidgeonHoles, The*

Sun, Tulip Tree Review, Westward Quarterly, and *Whatcom Writes* among others. Bellingham Repertory Dance, Snowdance Film Festival, and the Direct Short Online Film Festival have featured his work.

"String of Pearls" was previously published in *Noisy Water, Poetry from Whatcom County, WA.*

Poet and essayist **Betty Scott** lives in Bellingham, WA. Her writing adventures began with a newspaper column for *The Wenatchee World.* Her work has been published throughout the Pacific Northwest and British Columbia. *Central Heating,* poems of loss and recovery, encourages readers to celebrate and support the biodiversity of planet Earth. Published in 2017, *Central Heating* is available through Cave Moon Press. Scott enjoys performing her poems with guitarist and singer JP Falcon Grady.

Cameron Scott received an MFA from the University of Arizona before traveling around the dusty (and not so dusty) west. He spends his time as a fly fishing guide in the summers for Taylor Creek Fly Shop in Colorado and his winters in Oregon working for Fishtrap, a literary non-profit. His second book of poetry, *The Book of Cold Mountain,* won the Blue Light Book Award. If you have leftovers, he will eat them. www.writerfish.com

Carla Shafer's poems appear in *Whatcom Places II; Noisy Waters Anthology; Peace Poems,* a 2015 international poetry collection. A Sue C. Boynton Poetry winner, her chapbook is *Remembering the Path.* She founded Chuckanut Sandstone Writers Theater. Co-founder of World Peace Poets and honored as a Writers International Network (WIN) Poetry Ambassador. She holds a B.S. in English from Lewis and Clark College and an M.Ed. from Bank Street College (NYC). She lives in Bellingham, WA.

Elizabeth Shiller is a Youngstown, Ohio native who is finishing up a Masters in Communications at the University of Akron after attending Youngstown State University for Journalism (BA). She is kind of a *Jack of all Trades*. Elizabeth writes for FanFest.com, works in a cat shelter, coaches Color Guard, and is finishing out a year of service through AmeriCorps. Poetry has always been her passion and escape from her busy life style.

Aaron J. Silverberg has lived in the great PNW since 1988. He has produced two poetry books, *Thoreau's Chair* (2001) and *Diamonds Only Water Can Wear* (2007). He is forever grateful for the opulent beauty of this region.

Matthew Sisson's poetry has appeared in magazines and journals ranging from *JAMA, The Journal of The American Medical Association* to the *Harvard Review Online*. He has been nominated for a Pushcart Prized and his book *Please, Call Me Moby* was published by the Pecan Grove Press, St. Mary's University, San Antonio, Texas. He is the former poetry editor of the trade journal *Modern Steel Construction* and has read his work on NPR's *On Point with Tom Ashcroft*.

Douglas M. Smith is co-editor of *In Drought Time: Scenes From Rural and Small Town Life* (Mayapple Press, 2005). He was a finalist in the 2016 *Mudfish Magazine* poetry contest judged by Edward Hirsch. He was also a semi-finalist in the 2016 poetry book competition sponsored by *Concrete Wolf Press*. His poems have appeared in numerous journals including *Third Wednesday, The Slant,* and *Sweetwaters*. Doug's novel, *The Corridor*, details his experience as a Detroit community organizer.

Rick Smith is a clinical Psychologist specializing in brain damage and domestic violence; he practices in Rancho Cucamonga, Calif. Smith plays harmonica for The Mescal Sheiks and for Music Formula. He can be heard on the sound track of the Oscar nominated *Days of Heaven*. He's published widely; recent books include *Whispering In A Mad Dog's Ear* and *Hard Landing*, both from Lummox Press.

"Real Poetry" appears in *Whispering In A Mad Dog's Ear* (Lummox Press, 2014) and had previously been published in *Malpais Review* (2012).

Laurence Snydal is a poet, musician, and retired teacher. He has published more than a hundred poems in magazines such as *Caperock, Spillway, Columbia,* and *Steam Ticket*. His work has also appeared in many anthologies including *Visiting Frost, The Poets Grimm,* and *The Year's Best Fantasy and Horror*. Some of his poems have been performed in Baltimore and NYC. He lives in San Jose, CA, with his wife Susan.

Clemens Starck is a Princeton drop-out, a former merchant seaman, a retired union carpenter and construction foreman, and the author of six books of poems—including the award-winning *Journeyman's Wages* (1995). The others are: *Studying Russian on Company Time* (1999), *China Basin* (2002), *Traveling Incognito* (2004), *Rembrandt, Chainsaw* (2011), and *Old Dogs, New Tricks* (2016). He lives outside of Dallas in the foothills of the Coast Range in western Oregon. www.clemstarck.com

"Long Creek, Walla Walla" appears in the author's collection *Old Dogs, New Tricks* (2016).

Carol Steinhagen is a recovering English professor, having retired from Marietta College to try life as a poet. Though she loves having time to ruminate and compose, she has returned to school to take classes in such daunting subjects as physics and to teach in a learning and retirement program. Examples of recently published poems may be found in *Earth's Daughters, Perfume River Poetry Review,* and *Slant.*

Margo Taft Stever's book *Cracked Piano* will be published by CavanKerry Press in 2019. Her previous collections include *The Lunatic Ball,* Kattywompus Press, 2015; *The Hudson Line,* Main Street Rag, 2012; *Frozen Spring,* Mid-List Press First Series Award for Poetry, 2002; and *Reading the Night Sky,* Riverstone Poetry Chapbook Contest, 1996. She is the founder of The Hudson Valley Writers' Center and founding and current co-editor of Slapering Hol Press.

"Braids" was first published in *West Branch.* "Braids" also appeared in *Frozen Spring,* Margo Taft Stever, Mid-List Press First Series Award for Poetry, 2002.

Lisa Stice is a poet/mother/military spouse who received a BA in English literature from Mesa State College (now Colorado Mesa University) and an MFA in creative writing from the University of Alaska Anchorage. She currently lives in North Carolina with her husband, daughter, and dog. She is a Pushcart Prize nominee and the author of *Uniform* (Aldrich Press, 2016). Find out more about her and her publications at lisastice.wordpress.com and facebook.com/ LisaSticePoet.

Diane Stone, a former technical writer-editor, began writing as a child in Florida. Her work has been published in *Rattle, Comstock Review, Floating Bridge Review, Adanna, Embers and Flames, Main Street Rag,* among others. She won first place in the 2015 *Bacopa Literary Review* poetry contest. Diane and her husband have lived for 20 years on Whidbey Island, north of Seattle.

Marc Swan's poems have recently been published in *Sanskrit, Crannóg, Mudfish, Gargoyle, Passager, Nuclear Impact Anthology, Concho River Review,* and *Westerly,* among others. Tall-lighthouse Press in London, England published his last two poetry collections: *In a Distinct Minor Key* (2007) and *Simple Distraction* (2009). He lives with his wife Dd in Portland Maine.

"Standing Tall" was originally published in *Wormwood Review #127* in 1992.

Laura Sweeney facilitates Writers for Life in central Iowa. She represented the Iowa Arts Council at the First International Teaching Artist's Conference in Oslo, Norway. Her recent and forthcoming poems appear in *Folia, Yellow Chair Review, Wordrunner eChapbook, Balloons Lit. Journal, Red Savina Review, One Sentence Poems, Midwest Review, Main Street Rag, Canadian Woman Studies,* and the anthology *Nuclear Impact: Broken Atoms in Our Hands.* She is an associate editor for *Eastern Iowa Review.*

"Starry Night" originally appeared in the Main Street Rag anthology, *It's About Time.*

Tiffany L. Thomas is a dual MA/MFA graduate student at the University of Alaska, Fairbanks. She is a poetry editor for *Permafrost Magazine*, a freelance editor of engineering manuscripts, a second-year composition instructor, a volunteer ESL tutor, and, presumably, a poet. Her other work can be found in *Blinders Journal*, *Menacing Hedge*, and at the *Academy of American Poets*.

Ann Tweedy's first fulllength poetry book, *The Body's Alphabet* (Headmistress Press, 2016) was awarded a Bisexual Book Award and was a finalist for a Lambda Literary Award and a Golden Crown Literary Society Award. She has published two chapbooks and her work appears in numerous journals. She is a Pushcart Prize and Best of the Net Award nominee, an MFA candidate at Hamline University, a law professor, and an in-house attorney for the Muckleshoot Tribe. www.anntweedy.com.

"when she looks into my eyes" was first published in an online journal called *QP: queer poetry*.

Nature and wild landscapes, outdoor pursuits (mushing, hiking, canoeing), travel, and interesting writing prompts inspire **Lucy Tyrrell**'s poetry. She recently retired as research coordinator at Denali National Park and Preserve and moved back to Wisconsin after 16 years in Alaska—trading a big mountain (Denali) for a big lake (Lake Superior). Because she drinks only an occasional lime beer or weak gin and tonic, she watched YouTube videos to learn how to make a margarita.

Gail Tyson publishes poetry, nonfiction, and fiction. Her work has appeared in such journals as *Appalachian Heritage, Art Ascent, Big Muddy, Cloudbank, San Pedro River Review, Still Point Arts Quarterly*, and the anthology, *Unbroken Circle: Stories of Diversity in the South*. Gail lives in Roswell, Georgia and in a log cabin in the Cherokee National Forest, East Tennessee.

"Old-Time Round" appeared in *Still: The Journal* in February 2016.

Karen Vande Bossche is a poet and short story writer who teaches middle school in Bellingham, Washington. She was born in Illinois, raised in California, and is currently settled in the Pacific Northwest. Her publications are included in such journals as *River Poets Anthology, Crack the Spine, Sweet Tree Review,* and many others. Karen has been writing for over half a century and believes she has at least another half century worth of poems and stories to share.

Jerry Vaughn is a retired Pastor who lives in Lawrence, Kansas. He discovered the joys of Beer and Spam while on a trip to Germany. To avoid the high cost of food he carried a few cans of Spam with him. Finding that beer was cheaper than soda allowed him the chance to experience the wonderful virtues of Beer and Spam.

Dianalee Velie is the Poet Laureate of Newbury, New Hampshire where she lives and writes. A graduate of Sarah Lawrence College, she holds a Master of Arts in Writing from Manhattanville College. She has authored five poetry books: *Glass House, First Edition, The Many Roads to Paradise, The Alchemy of Desire, Ever After,* and a short story collection *Soul Proprietorship: Women in Search of Their Souls.* She is a founder of the John Hay Poetry Society.

Jack Vian is a poet and writer who lives and works within the razor-wire shadows of the Texas Parole Board's amber-coated archipelago of vengeance and woe. He follows the Dharma, practices Yoga, and mentors those seeking release. His work has appeared in such places as *Rattle, Colere, Poet Lore, The Chiron Review,* and *Gemini Magazine,* among many others. He would be very pleased if he could one day share a drink with you. Email: jackvianjr@gmail.com

Sam Wagner started by collecting beer labels, trying new beers for the sake of the label, and eventually for the sake of the beer. Then he worked at breweries, writing ad copy and tending bar. Eventually, after consuming the delicious history, science, and art of beer, Sam felt ready to indulge the adage, "write what you know."

"Death at City Tavern" and "The Beer Not Dranken" originally appeared in *The Poetry of Beer,* a self-published poetry collection entirely about beer.

Jeff Walt is a 2018 resident artist at The Fairhope Center for the Writing Arts in Alabama. His work has appeared in *Los Angeles Review, Alligator Juniper, The Sun, Connecticut Review, Inkwell, New Millennium Writings, The Good Men Project, Harpur Palate, Cream City Review, The Ledge,* and *Slipstream.* www.jeffwalt.com.

"Becoming a Regular" first appeared in the chapbook, *Soot* (Seven Kitchens Press, 2010), co-winner of the Keystone Chapbook Prize.
"Kitchen Music" was chosen by Marie Howe to receive the only Honorable Mention in the Manhattenville College 5th Annual *Inkwell* Magazine Poetry Competition and was published in the Spring 2002 issue.

Michael Waters' books include *Celestial Joyride* (2016), *Gospel Night* (2011), and *Darling Vulgarity* (2006—*Los Angeles Times* Book Prize finalist). He has co-edited *Contemporary American Poetry* (Houghton Mifflin, 2006) and *Perfect in Their Art: Poems on Boxing from Homer to Ali* (Southern Illinois UP, 2003). Recipient of five Pushcart Prizes, fellowships from the NEA, Fulbright Foundation, and NJ State Council on the Arts, Waters teaches at Monmouth University and in the Drew University MFA Program.

"Classic Cocktail" first appeared in *The Gettysburg Review*.

Poet Laureate *emerita* for the small seaside town of Rockport, Massachusetts, **Suellen Wedmore** has been awarded first place in both the *Writer's Digest's* Rhyming Poem and the Non-Rhyming Poem Contests. Her chapbook *Deployed* won the Grayson Press annual contest, her chapbook *On Marriage and Other Parallel Universes* was published by Finishing Line Press, and her chapbook *Mind the Light* won a first place in Quill's Press's "Women on the Edge" contest. Three of her poems have been nominated for a Pushcart Prize.

"Martini" was previously published in *Jabberwock Review* (Winter 2012).

Sarah Brown Weitzman, a National Endowment for the Arts Fellow in Poetry and Pushcart prize nominee, has been published in hundreds of journals and anthologies including *Rosebud, The New Ohio Review, Poet & Critic, The North American Review, Rattle, Mid-American Review, The Macguffin, Poet Lore*, etc. A departure from poetry, her fourth book, *Herman And The Ice Witch*, is a children's novel published by Main Street Rag.

"Bourbon" was previously published in *Pembroke Magazine*, Vol. 44, 2012.

Daniel Weldon is a Native of the Pacific Northwest. He earned his BA degree in Communications from Cal Poly and a MBA from George Fox University. When not distilling experiences into short poetry pieces, he works in commercial finance and balances his work by getting outdoors, supporting local music, or binge-watching the latest crime procedural series. He lives with his partner, Emily, and their two dogs, Olive Josephine and Hero John, in Portland, OR.

Patricia Wellingham-Jones lives on a creek in rural northern California where she enjoys writing about the things that happen around her – past and present. A retired RN, psychology researcher and editor/writer/publisher, she has a special interest in healing writing, with poems recently in *The Widow's Handbook* (Kent State University Press). Chapbooks include *Don't Turn Away: poems about breast cancer, End-Cycle: poems about caregiving, Apple Blossoms at Eye Level, Voices on the Land,* and *Hormone Stew.*

"Cocktail Hour" was first published in *End-Cycle*, 2007.

Ed Werstein, from Milwaukee, spent many years in manufacturing and union activity before his muse awoke and dragged herself out of bed. He advocates for peace and against corporate power. His poetry has appeared in *Stoneboat Literary Journal, Verse Wisconsin, Blue Collar Review, Gyroscope Review, Naugatuck River Review,* and several other publications. He is a regional

VP of the Wisconsin Fellowship of Poets (www.wfop.org). His chapbook *Who Are We Then?* was published by Partisan Press.

Richard Widerkehr holds an M.A. from Columbia University and won two Hopwood first prizes for poetry from the University of Michigan. He has published three books of poems: *In the Presence of Absence* (MoonPath Press), *The Way Home* (Plain View Press), and *Her Story of Fire* (Egress Studio Press), two chapbooks, and a novel *Sedimental Journey* (Tarragon Books). His poems appear in *Rattle, Arts and Letters,* and *Cirque.* He's a poetry editor at *Shark Reef Review.*

"At Playa Catalonia" appears in *In the Presence of Absence* (MoonPath Press, 2017).

Steve Wilson's poetry has appeared in journals nationwide, including *Beloit Poetry Journal, New American Writing, Cimarron Review, North American Review, New Orleans Review,* and *New Letters.* He is the author of three collections of poetry, most recently *The Lost Seventh*; and editor of *The Anatomy of Water: Contemporary American Prose Poetry.* He lives in San Marcos, Texas and teaches at Texas State University.

"Little Poem for Edward Gorey" first appeared in *The Beloit Poetry Journal.*

Koon Woon was born in China in 1949 and immigrated to the US in 1960. He earned a BA at Antioch University Seattle and an MLS degree from Fort Hays State University in literary arts. His books are *The Truth in Rented Rooms* and *Water Chasing Water,* both from Kaya

Press. He has received a Pen Oakland and an American Book Award for his poetry. He lives in Seattle where he hosts the online journal *Five Willows Literary Review* and operates the literary press Goldfish Press.

Frank Wright's first professional writing job was as a reporter for a small-town daily newspaper. Over the years, he has written advertising copy, articles for professional publications, film scripts, and furniture assembly instructions. From time-to-time he has written love poems to his paramour. Now, retired from teaching, he paints, and writes fiction.

Jeanne Yeasting is a writer and a visual artist. She is an admirer of life's absurdities and the extraordinariness of the ordinary. She lives and teaches in Bellingham, Washington. She has never met a writing prompt she didn't like.

Author Index

A

B

C

Sweeney, Laura 203, 235, 288

CPSIA information can be obtained
at www.ICGtesting.com
Printed in the USA
FSHW011249311018
53450FS